IMAGES AND SYMBOLS

IMAGES AND SYMBOLS

*Studies in
Religious Symbolism*

MIRCEA ELIADE

Translated by
PHILIP MAIRET

A SEARCH BOOK: SHEED AND WARD
NEW YORK

Library of Congress Catalog Card Number 61-7290

*This book was
originally published in France by Gallimard
under the title of*
IMAGES ET SYMBOLES

Search Book edition, 1969

To the memory of my father
GHÉORGHÉ ELIADE
1870–1951

CONTENTS

Contents

Foreword

The surprising popularity of psychoanalysis has made the fortunes of certain key-words: image, symbol and symbolism have now become current coin. At the same time, systematic research devoted to the mechanisms of "primitive mentality" has revealed the importance of symbolism in archaic thinking and also the fundamental part it plays in the life of any and every primitive society. The obsolescence of "scientism" in philosophy, the revival of interest in religion since the first world war, many poetic developments and, above all, the researches of surrealism (with the rediscovery of occultism, of the "black" literature, of "the absurd", etc.) have, on various levels and with unequal effects, drawn the attention of the public in general to the symbol, regarded as an autonomous mode of cognition. The development in question is a part of the reaction against the nineteenth century's rationalism, positivism and scientism which became such a marked characteristic of the second quarter of the twentieth. But this conversion to the various symbolisms is not really a "discovery" to be credited to the modern world: in restoring the symbol to its status as an instrument of knowledge, our world is only returning to a point of view that was general in Europe until the eighteenth century and is, moreover, connatural to the other, non-European cultures, whether "historic" (like those of Asia or Central America for instance) or archaic and "primitive".

It is noteworthy that the invasion of Western Europe by symbolism coincides with the arrival of Asia on the horizon of history; an advent which, initiated by the revolution of Sun Yat Sen, has been unmistakably affirmed during the last few years.

Meanwhile, ethnic groups which until now had no place in world history except for glimpses and passing allusions (such as the Oceanians, Africans and others) are preparing in their turn to enter into the great currents of contemporary history and are already impatient to do so. Not that there is any causal connection whatever between the rising of the "exotic" or "archaic" world above the horizon of history and the return to favour, in Europe, of symbolic knowledge. But the fact is that this synchronism is particularly fortunate: one may well ask how else the positivistic and materialistic Europe of the nineteenth century would have been able to maintain a spiritual conversation with "exotic" cultures, all of which without exception are devoted to ways of thought that are alien to empiricism or positivism. This gives us at least some grounds for hope that Europe will not remain paralysed before the images and symbols which, in that exotic world, either take the place of our concepts or take them up and extend them. It is a striking fact that, of all our modern European spirituality, two things alone *really* interest the non-European worlds: Christianity and Communism. Both of these, in different ways and upon clearly opposed grounds, are soteriologies—doctrines of salvation—and therefore deal in "symbols" and "myths" upon a scale without parallel except among non-European humanity.[1]

A fortunate conjunction in time, as we said, has enabled Western Europe to rediscover the cognitive value of the symbol at the moment when Europeans are no longer the only peoples to "make history", and when European culture, unless it shuts itself off into a sterilising provincialism, will be obliged to reckon with

[1] This is an extreme simplification, for it refers to an aspect of things which it is impossible for us to enter upon in this chapter. In regard to the soteriological myths and symbols of communism it is evident that, whatever reservations we make about the Marxist *élite* and leadership, the masses in sympathy are stimulated and driven by slogans such as liberation, freedom, peace, elimination of social conflicts, abolition of State exploitation and of privileged classes, etc.; slogans whose mythical structure and function need no further demonstration.

other ways of knowing and other scales of values than its own. In this respect, all the discoveries and successive fashions concerned with the irrational, with the unconscious, with symbolisms, poetic experience, exotic and non-representational art, etc., have been, indirectly, of service to the West as preparations for a more living and therefore a deeper understanding of non-European values, and in particular for a dialogue with the non-European peoples. One has only to reflect upon the attitude that nineteenth-century ethnography took up towards its subject, and above all to consider the results of its researches, to measure the progress made by ethnography during the last thirty years. The ethnologist of today has not only grasped the importance of symbolism in archaic thinking but has seen its intrinsic coherence, its validity, its speculative audacity, its "nobility".

Better still: today we are well on the way to an understanding of one thing of which the nineteenth century had not even a presentiment—that the symbol, the myth and the image are of the very substance of the spiritual life, that they may become disguised, mutilated or degraded, but are never extirpated. It would be well worth while to study the survival of the great myths throughout the nineteenth century: one would then see how they were humbled, minimised, condemned to incessant change of form, and yet survived that hibernation, thanks chiefly to literature.[2] Thus it is that the myth of the Earthly Paradise has survived until today, in adapted form as an "Oceanian paradise"; for the last hundred and fifty years all the great European literatures have vied with each other in exalting the paradisiac islands of the Pacific Ocean, havens of all happiness, although the reality was very different—"flat and monotonous landscapes, unhealthy climates, ugly and obese women", etc. But the Image of this "Oceanian paradise" remained proof against geographical or any other realities. What had objective realities to do with the "Oceanian

[2] What an inspiring study it would be, to bring to light the real spiritual function of the nineteenth century novel which, despite all scientific, realistic or social "formulas", remained the great repository of degraded myths!

paradise"? This was something of a theological order: it had received, assimilated and readapted all the paradisiac images repressed by positivism and scientism. The Earthly Paradise still believed in by Christopher Columbus (did he not fancy he had discovered it?) turned into a South Sea island in the nineteenth century, but its function in the economy of the human psyche remained the same: over there, in the "island", in that "paradise", existence unfolded itself outside Time and History; man was happy, free and unconditioned; he did not have to work for his living; the women were young, eternally beautiful, and no "law" hung heavily over their loves. Even nudity, in that distant isle, recovered its metaphysical meaning—that of perfect humanity, of Adam before the Fall.[3] Geographical "reality" might give the lie to that paradisiac landscape, ugly and corpulent women might confront the travellers' eyes; but these they did not see; each one saw only the image he had brought with him.

SYMBOLISM AND PSYCHOANALYSIS

Symbolic thinking is not the exclusive privilege of the child, of the poet or of the unbalanced mind: it is consubstantial with human existence, it comes before language and discursive reason. The symbol reveals certain aspects of reality—the deepest aspects —which defy any other means of knowledge. Images, symbols and myths are not irresponsible creations of the psyche; they respond to a need and fulfil a function, that of bringing to light the most hidden modalities of being. Consequently, the study of them enables us to reach a better understanding of man—of man "as he is", before he has come to terms with the conditions of History. Every historical man carries on, within himself, a great deal of prehistoric humanity. That, indeed, is a point that was never quite

[3] To the symbolism of the island and of nudity in the work of one of the great poets of the nineteenth century, Mihail Eminescu, we have devoted a study that was published in 1938. See our *Insula lui Euthanasius*, Bucharest, 1943, pp. 5-18.

forgotten even in the most inclement days of positivism; for who knows better than a positivist that man is an "animal", defined and ruled by the same instincts as his brothers, the animals? That correct but incomplete description served as an exclusive frame of reference. But today we are beginning to see that the non-historical portion of every human being does not simply merge into the animal kingdom, as in the nineteenth century so many thought it did, nor ultimately into "Life"; but that, on the contrary, it bifurcates and rises right above Life. This non-historical part of the human being wears, like a medal, the imprinted memory of a richer, a more complete and almost beatific existence. When a historically conditioned being—for instance, an Occidental of our own days—allows himself to be invaded by the non-historical part of himself (which happens to him much oftener and more completely than he imagines), this is not necessarily a retrogression towards the animal stage of humanity or a redescent towards the deepest sources of organic life. Often he is re-entering, by means of the images and the symbols that then come into play, a paradisiac stage of primordial humanity (whatever its concrete existence may then have been; for this "primordial man" is admittedly an archetype never fully "realisable" in any human existence at all). In escaping from his historicity, man does not abdicate his status as a human being or abandon himself to "animality": he recovers the language, and sometimes the experience, of a "lost paradise". Dreams, waking dreams, the images of his nostalgias and of his enthusiasms, etc., are so many forces that may project the historically-conditioned human being into a spiritual world that is infinitely richer than the closed world of his own "historic moment".

According to the surrealists, any man might become a poet: he need only know how to give himself up to automatic writing. Their poetic technique is fully justifiable from sound psychological doctrine. The "unconscious", as it is called, is far more "poetic"—and, let us add, more "philosophic", more "mythic"—than the conscious. It is not always necessary to know mythology

in order to live out the great mythical themes. This is well known
to psychologists, who discover the most beautiful mythologies
in the "waking dreams" of their patients. For the unconscious is
not haunted by monsters only: the gods, the goddesses, the heroes
and the fairies dwell there too; moreover, the monsters of the unconscious are themselves mythological, seeing that they continue
to fulfil the same functions that they fulfilled in all the mythologies—in the last analysis, that of helping man to liberate himself, to complete his initiation.

The brutal language of Freud and his orthodox disciples has
often irritated *bien pensants* readers. In fact, however, that
brutality of language arises from a misunderstanding: it is not the
sexuality in itself that is annoying, it is the ideology that Freud
built upon his "pure sexuality". Fascinated by his mission—he
believed himself to be the first Awakened One, whereas he was
only the last of the Positivists—Freud could not bring himself to
see that sexuality never has been "pure", that everywhere and
always it is a polyvalent function whose primary and perhaps
supreme valency is the cosmological function: so that to translate
a psychic situation into sexual terms is by no means to belittle it;
for, except in the modern world, sexuality has everywhere and
always been a hierophany, and the sexual act an integral action
(therefore also a means to knowledge).

The attraction that the male infant feels towards its mother,
and its corollary the Œdipus complex, are only "shocking" in so
far as they are analysed *as such*; instead of being presented as they
should be, *as so much imagery*. For it is the Image of the Mother
that is really in question, and not this or that mother *hic et nunc*, as
Freud gives one to understand. It is the Image of the Mother
which reveals—and which *alone can reveal*—her reality and her
functions, at once cosmological, anthropological and psychological.[4] To "translate" the images into concrete terms is an

[4] The greatest merit of C. G. Jung is that he has gone further than Freudian
psychoanalysis *on the plane of psychology itself*, and has thus restored the spiritual
significance of the Image.

operation devoid of meaning: the images comprise, it is true, all those allusions to the "concrete" that Freud has brought to light, but the reality that they are trying to signify cannot be reduced to such "concrete" references. The "origin" of the Images, also, is a problem that is beside the point; it is as though one were to dispute the truth of mathematics on the pretext that the "historical discovery" of geometry emerged from the great works undertaken by the ancient Egyptians for the canalisation of the Delta.

Philosophically, these problems of the "origin" and of the "true interpretation" of the Images are pointless. We need only remember that the attraction to the mother, if we interpret it on the plane of the immediate and "concrete"—like the desire to possess one's own mother—can *never tell us anything more than what it says*; whereas, if we take account of the fact that what is in question is the Image of the Mother, this desire means many things at once, for it is the desire to re-enter into the bliss of living Matter that is still "unformed", with all its possible lines of development, cosmological, anthropological, etc. For, as we have said and as the following pages will show, Images by their very structure are *multivalent*. If the mind makes use of images to grasp the ultimate reality of things, it is just because reality manifests itself in contradictory ways and therefore cannot be expressed in concepts. (We know what desperate efforts have been made by various theologies and metaphysics, oriental as well as occidental, to give expression to the *coincidentia oppositorum*—a mode of being that is readily, and also abundantly, conveyed by images and symbols.) It is therefore the image as such, as a whole bundle of meanings, that is *true*, and not any *one* of its meanings, nor one alone of its many frames of reference. To translate an image into a concrete terminology by restricting it to any one of its frames of reference is to do worse than mutilate it—it is to annihilate, to annul it as an instrument of cognition.

We are not unaware that in certain cases the psyche may fixate an image on one single frame of reference—that of the "concrete"; but this is already a proof of psychic disequilibrium. No doubt there are cases in which the Image of the Mother is no more than an incestuous desire for the actual mother; but psychologists are in agreement in seeing such a carnal interpretation of the symbol as a sign of psychic crisis. Upon the actual plane of dialectic of the image, any exclusive reduction is an aberration. The history of religions, too, abounds in unilateral and therefore aberrant interpretations of symbols. One could hardly adduce a single great religious symbol whose history is not that of a tragic succession of innumerable "falls". There is no heresy so monstrous or orgy so infernal, no religious cruelty, folly, absurdity, or religious magic so insane, that it may not be "justified" in its very principle by some false—*because partial and incomplete*—interpretation of a grandiose symbolism.[5]

Fundamentalism

THE SURVIVAL OF IMAGES

It is not necessary, however, to appeal to the discoveries of depth-psychology or the surrealist techniques of automatic writing in order to prove the subconscious survival, in modern man, of a mythology that is ever abundant and, in our view, of a spiritual authenticity superior to his "conscious" living. We do not need to rely on the poets or psychiatry for confirmation of the actuality and power of images and symbols. The most commonplace existence swarms with images, the most "realistic" man lives by them. Let us repeat—and what follows will richly illustrate this—that symbols never disappear from the *reality* of the psyche. The aspect of them may change, but their function remains the same; one has only to look behind their latest masks.

The most abject "nostalgia" discloses the "nostalgia for Paradise". The images of the "oceanic paradise" that we have mentioned haunt our novels as well as our films. (Who was it said of the cinema that it was "the factory of dreams"?) We might just as well analyse the images suddenly released by any sort of music,

[5] See our *Patterns in Comparative Religion*, London-New York, 1958, pp. 354 ff., *et passim*.

sometimes by the most sentimental song; and we should find that these images express the nostalgia for a mythicised past transformed into an archetype, and that this "past" signifies not only regrets for a vanished time but countless other meanings; it expresses all that might have been but was not, the sadness of all existence, which *is* only by ceasing to be something else; regrets that one does not live in the country or in the times evoked by the song (whatever the local or historical colouring may be—the Russia of the balalaikas, the gorgeous East, the Haiti of the films, the life of the American millionaire, the exotic prince, etc.)—in short, the longing for something *altogether different* from the present instant; something in fact inaccessible or irretrievably lost: "Paradise" itself.

What is important about these images of the nostalgia for paradise is that they always express more than the subject who has experienced them could convey in words. Moreover, most human beings would be incapable of describing them, not because they are less intelligent than the others, but because they do not attach over-much importance to our analytical language. Such images bring men together, however, more effectively and more genuinely than any analytical language. Indeed, if an ultimate solidarity of the whole human race does exist, it can be felt and "activated" only at the level of the Images (we do not say "of the subconscious" for we have no proof that there may not also be a transconscious).

Men have paid too little attention to such "nostalgias"; they have not cared to recognise them as anything more than insignificant psychic by-products; or at the most, have agreed that they may be of interest in certain inquiries into the forms of psychic evasion. But the nostalgias are sometimes charged with meanings that concern man's actual situation; and this entitles them to consideration by the philosopher as much as by the theologian. Still, they were not taken seriously; they were felt to be "frivolous". An image of Paradise Lost suddenly evoked by the music of an accordion?—what a compromising subject for a study! This was to forget that the life of modern man is swarming with half-forgotten myths, decaying hierophanies and secularised symbols. The progressive de-sacralisation of modern man has altered the content of his spiritual life without breaking the matrices of his imagination: a quantity of mythological litter still lingers in the ill-controlled zones of the mind.

Moreover, the most "noble" part of a modern man's consciousness is less "spiritual" than one is usually inclined to think. A brief analysis would discover that this "noble" or "higher" sphere of consciousness contained a few bookish reminiscences, a number of prejudices of various kinds (religious, moral, social, æsthetic, etc.), some ready-made ideas about the "meaning of life", "ultimate reality" and so forth. But beware of looking further, for what has become of the myth of the Lost Paradise, for instance, or the Image of the perfect Man, the mystery of Woman and of Love, etc.! All these are to be found (but how desecrated, degraded and artificialised!) among many other things in the semi-conscious flux of the most down-to-earth existence—in its waking dreams, its fits of melancholy, in the free play of images when consciousness is "taking time off" (in the street, the underground railway or elsewhere), and in all kinds of distractions and amusements. There it lies hidden, the whole treasury of myths, "laicised" and "modernised". What has happened to the images is what happens, as Freud has shown us, in the case of over-crude allusions to sexual realities—they have changed their "form". In order to survive, the Images take on "familiar" shapes.

They are of no less interest for all that. These degraded images present to us the only possible point of departure for the spiritual renewal of modern man. It is of the greatest importance, we believe, to rediscover a whole mythology, if not a theology, still concealed in the most ordinary, everyday life of contemporary man; it will depend upon himself whether he can work his way back to the source and rediscover the profound meanings of all these faded images and damaged myths. But let no one object that these relics are of no interest to modern man, that they belong to a "superstitious past" happily liquidated by the nineteenth century . . . or that it is all right for poets, children and the people in the Tube to satiate themselves with nostalgias and images, but for goodness' sake let serious people go on thinking and "making history". Such a separation between the "serious things of life" and "dreams" does not correspond with reality. Modern man is free to despise mythologies and theologies, but that will not prevent his continuing to feed upon decayed myths and degraded images. The most terrible historical crisis of the modern world— the second world war and all that has followed from it—has effectually demonstrated that the extirpation of myths and symbols is illusory. Even in the most desperate of "historical situations" (in the trenches of Stalingrad, in both Nazi and Soviet concentration camps) men and women have sung ballads and listened to stories, even giving up a part of their meagre rations to to obtain them; and these stories were but projections of the myths, these ballads were filled with "nostalgias". All that essential and indescribable part of man that is called *imagination* dwells in realms of symbolism and still lives upon archaic myths and theologies.[6]

It depends, as we said, upon modern man—to "reawaken" the inestimable treasure of images that he bears within him; and to reawaken the images so as to contemplate them in their pristine purity and assimilate their message. Popular wisdom has many a time given expression to the importance of imagination

[6] See the rich and penetrating analyses by Gaston Bachelard in his works on the "imagination of matter"—*La Psychanalyse du Feu, L'Eau et les Rêves, L'Air et les Songes, La Terre et les Rêveries*, 2 vols., Paris, 1939-1948. G. Bachelard bases his views mainly upon poetry and dreams, and secondarily upon folk-lore; but one could easily show how dreams and poetic imagery are continuous with sacred symbolism and archaic mythologies. With regard to the images of Water and the Earth, such as pervade dreams and literature, cf. the chapters on the hierophanies and the aquatic and telluric symbolisms in our *Patterns in Comparative Religion*, pp. 188 ff., 239 ff.

for the very health of the individual and for the balance and richness of his inner life. In some modern languages the man who
"lacks imagination" is still pitied as a limited, second-rate and un-
happy being. The psychologists, C. G. Jung among others of the
first rank, have shown us how much the dramas of the modern
world proceed from a profound disequilibrium of the psyche,
individual as well as collective, brought about largely by a progressive sterilisation of the imagination. To "have imagination"
is to enjoy a richness of interior life, an uninterrupted and spontaneous flow of images. But spontaneity does not mean arbitrary
invention. Etymologically, "imagination" is related to both
imago—a representation or imitation—and *imitor*, to imitate or
reproduce. And for once, etymology is in accord with both
psychological realities and spiritual truth. The imagination
imitates the exemplary models—the Images—reproduces, re-
actualises and repeats them without end. To have imagination is
to be able to see the world in its totality, for the power and the
mission of the Images is to *show* all that remains refractory to the
concept: hence the disfavour and failure of the man "without
imagination"; he is cut off from the deeper reality of life and from
his own soul.

In recalling these principles we were trying to show that the
study of symbolism is not a work of pure and simple erudition,
but one that concerns, at least indirectly, the knowledge of man
himself: in short, that it has something to say to anyone who is
speaking of a new humanism or a new anthropology. Doubtless,
such a study of the symbolisms will be of real use only when it is
carried on in collaboration. Literary æsthetics, psychology and
philosophical anthropology ought to take account of the findings
of the history of religions, of ethnology and folk-lore. It is
primarily with the psychologists and literary critics in mind that
we have published this book. The historian of religions is in a
better position than anyone else to promote the knowledge of
symbols, his documents being at once more comprehensive and
more coherent than those at the disposal of the psychologist or the

literary critic; they are drawn from the very sources of symbolical thinking. It is in the history of religions that we meet with the "archetypes", of which only approximate variants are dealt with by psychologists and literary critics.

THE PLAN OF THE BOOK

The first four chapters of this book were written at different times and for different kinds of readers.[7] Chapters I and II are accompanied by a minimum of notes: the material upon which they are based had already been incorporated, either in our own previous works or those of other investigators. Chapters III and IV, however, call for a certain number of notes and references. The material that is brought together in them is in itself enough to make them useful monographs, apart from the interpretation that we have proposed. The last chapter, which at the same time serves as a general conclusion, is also presented with a restricted bibliographic apparatus. The subject it deals with was too vast to permit of an exposition that would be both carefully documented and extremely concise.

With the exception of the last chapter, the various studies that follow were not composed to constitute a book: each of them was, however, in the author's mind, an answer to one and the same problem—namely, that of the structure of religious symbolism. Each chapter presents one symbolism or one family of symbols, although the way in which they are envisaged may vary from one to another. The symbolism of the "Centre", which is studied in the first chapter, and extends the results of some other, previous studies, is synthetically expounded, without regard to the complications of "history". The first part of this chapter

[7] The fourth chapter dates back to 1938 (see *Zalmoxis*, Vol. II, pp. 131 ff.); the third to 1946 (see the *Revue de l'Histoire des Religions*, Vol. CXXXIV, July-December, 1947-8, pp. 5 ff.). The substance of Chaps. I and II was the subject of our lectures at Ascona, 1950-51 (see the *Eranos Jahrbuch*, Vols. XIX and XX); and of an article in the *Journal of Psychology*.

states, indeed, the problem of the validity of such a comprehensive treatment of the symbol, and briefly indicates the relations between psychology and the history of religions.

The second chapter analyses the symbolism of Time and of the "going out of Time" in one and the same cultural area—that of ancient India. The third chapter deals with the symbolism of knots, upon two complementary planes: after confining itself chiefly to the Indo-Europeans, by using the researches of Georges Dumézil, it endeavours to compare these data with the parallel symbolisms of other archaic cultures. It is in this chapter above all that we shall measure the advantages and the limitations both of historical investigation and of morphological analysis; and thus come to a better understanding of the necessity of making successive use of both these complementary methods. The fourth chapter, devoted to a group of associated symbols (Moon—Water—Fertility, etc.) constitutes a description of morphological type, intended to elucidate the structures. Finally, the last chapter resumes the findings of all these inquiries from different standpoints, with a view to a systematic integration of magicoreligious symbolism.

The psychologist will be chiefly interested in the first two chapters and the last. The reader who is pressed for time may excuse himself from reading all of the analyses and the references given in Chapters III and IV. We have not, however, thought fit to suppress these notes. The danger with studies of symbolism is that of precipitate generalisation. Laymen are inclined to content themselves with the first documents that come to their notice and to construct audacious "general" interpretations of the symbolisms. We have been careful to present at least two examples of analysis of the symbols discussed, in order to show how subtle and complex these things really are. On the other hand, we wanted to place some fairly full material at the disposal of psychologists and literary critics, and indeed of philosophers, to enable them to use it, if need be, to their own ends. It is not uncommon, in the books of psychologists and literary critics, to find a documentation that is worse than insufficient—frankly faulty: the books from which they have taken their material are, oftener than not, the products of amateurs without a critical sense, or of isolated "theorists".[8] The non-specialists reply, with some reason, that they cannot do the work of ethnologists and historians of religions, that they have neither the means nor the leisure to undertake long-term researches, and that they are obliged to do their best with such "general" works as come to hand. The misfortune is that, most of the time, the non-specialists fall for the most mediocre of these

---

[8] Freud thought he had discovered the "origin" of religions in the Œdipus complex born of a primordial parricide—a parricide ritually repeated in the "totemic sacrifices". He elaborated his theory—which appears still to retain the approbation of the psychoanalysts—in 1911-1912, by making use of the hypothesis of the "primordial horde" of Atkinson, and that of the "totemic sacrifice-communion" of Robertson Smith. At the time when Freud was elaborating his explanation of the religious sentiment, and imagined that he had found the "origin" of religion, the two hypotheses mentioned no longer enjoyed any credit among competent ethnologists and historians of religions. But although Freud had read Frazer and knew the conclusions that Frazer had come to— namely, the *non-universality* of totemism as a social-religious phenomenon (it is unknown among a number of primitive tribes) and the *extreme rarity* of the "sacrifice-communions" (only four cases—and those unequally confirmed— out of several hundreds of totemic tribes!), nevertheless *Totem and Tabu* appeared in book form in 1913 and since then has been continually republished and translated into numerous languages . . . (One might invoke, in defence of Freud, the appearance in 1912 of the famous book by Émile Durkheim, *Les formes élémentaires de la vie religieuse*, a book that is precious in several respects, sometimes almost a work of genius, but tiresomely lacking in foundation. Considerably better informed than Freud, Durkheim fell into the same error of method, by trying to find the "origin" of religions in totemism. This eminent master would have done better had he taken into account the work of his ethnological and anthropological colleagues who had already sufficiently proved that totemism *does not represent the most ancient stratum of the Australian religions* and, furthermore, that it is *absent from numerous archaic cultures* dispersed throughout the world.)

"general works"; and, even when they have better luck, they sometimes happen to read badly or too hastily.

That is why we have resisted the temptation to suppress the bibliographical apparatus:[9] perhaps some non-specialists may feel the need of making personal contact with the mass of works on ethnology and the history of religions, instead of taking their nourishment from the sorry, out-of-date lucubrations of dilettanti or "theorists" who have been chiefly concerned to illustrate their own generalisations. Psychological literature, especially that produced by psychoanalysis, will have familiarised the reader with the prolixity of its expositions of individual "case-histories". One volume published in England has seven hundred pages on the "dream mythology" of a single individual! The psychologists are in agreement about the indispensability of exposition *in extenso* of each particular case, and when they resign themselves to its abbreviation, it is almost always with reluctance: their ideal would be to publish complete dossiers. With much greater reason ought one to take the same course when studying a symbolism: we need to present it in general outline, but also with all its subtleties, variants and uncertainties.

The central and the most arduous problem remains, obviously, that of interpretation. In principle, one can always question the validity of a hermeneutic study. By multiple cross references between what is clearly established (texts, rituals and figured monuments) and semi-veiled allusions, we can demonstrate, bit by bit, what this or that symbol "means". But we can also state the problem in another way: do those who are making use of the symbols take all their theoretical implications into account? When, for instance, in studying the implications of the cosmic Tree, we say that the Tree is situated at the "Centre of the World", do we mean that all the individuals belonging to societies which know of such Trees are equally aware of the complete symbolism of the "Centre"? But the validity of the symbol con-

---

[9] We have lightened it, however, for the purposes of the present English translation.

sidered as a form of knowledge does not depend upon any individual's degree of understanding. Texts and figured monuments provide us with abundant proof that for some, at least, of the individuals of an archaic society the symbolism of the "Centre" was transparent in its totality; the rest of the society remaining content to "participate" in the symbolism. Moreover, it is not easy to draw the limits of such a participation, for it varies in function with an indefinite number of factors. All we can say is that the *actualisation* of a symbol is not automatic; it occurs in relation to the tensions and vicissitudes of the social life, and, finally, with the cosmic rhythms.

But whatever eclipses or aberrations a symbolism may undergo from the very fact that it is *lived*, this does not lessen the validity of its hermeneutics. To take an illustration from another order of realities—in order to understand the symbolism of the *Divina Commedia*, is it necessary to ask what its millions of readers, distributed all over the globe, have made of that difficult book; or should we not rather ask what Dante himself felt and thought when writing it? In the case of poetic works of a freer kind—I mean those that depend more directly upon "inspiration", such as the productions of German romanticism—we have not even the right to restrict ourselves to what the authors thought about their own creations, if we would interpret the symbolism involved in them. The fact is that in most cases an author does not understand all the meaning of his work. Archaic symbolisms reappear spontaneously, even in the works of "realist" authors who know nothing about such symbols.

Moreover, this controversy over the legitimate limits of the hermeneutic appraisals of symbols is quite unprofitable. We have seen that myths decay and symbols become secularised, but that they never disappear, even in the most positivist of civilisations, that of the nineteenth century. Symbols and myths come from such depths: they are part and parcel of the human being, and it is impossible that they should not be found again in any and every existential situation of man in the Cosmos.

I

Symbolism of the " Centre "

Many laymen envy the vocation of the historian of religions.
What nobler or more rewarding occupation could there be than
to frequent the great mystics of all the religions, to live among
symbols and mysteries, to read and understand the myths of all
the nations? The layman imagines that a historian of religions
must be equally at home with the Greek or the Egyptian mythology, with the authentic teaching of the Buddha, the Taoist
mysteries or the secret rites of initiation in archaic societies. Perhaps laymen are not altogether wrong in thinking that the
historian of religions is immersed in vast and genuine problems,
engaged in the decipherment of the most impressive symbols and
the most complex and lofty myths from the immense mass of
material that offers itself to him. Yet in fact the situation is quite
different. A good many historians of religions are so absorbed in
their special studies that they know little more about the Greek or
Egyptian mythologies, or the Buddha's teaching, or the Taoist or
shamanic techniques, than any amateur who has known how to
direct his reading. Most of them are really familiar with only one
poor little sector of the immense domain of religious history.
And, unhappily, even this modest sector is, more often than not,
but superficially exploited by the decipherment, editing and
translation of texts, historical monographs or the cataloguing of
monuments, etc. Confined to an inevitably limited subject, the
historian of religions often has a feeling that he has sacrificed the

fine spiritual career of his youthful dreams to the dull duty of scientific probity.

But the excessive scientific probity of his output has ended by alienating him from the cultured public. Except for quite rare exceptions, the historians of religions are not read outside the restricted circles of their colleagues and disciples. The public no longer reads their books, either because they are too technical or too dull; in short because they awaken no spiritual interest. By force of hearing it repeated—as it was, for instance, by Sir James Frazer throughout some twenty thousand pages—that everything thought, imagined or desired by man in archaic societies, all his myths and rites, all his gods and religious experiences, are nothing but a monstrous accumulation of madnesses, cruelties and superstitions now happily abolished by the progress of mankind—by dint of listening almost always to the same thing, the public has at last let itself be convinced, and has ceased to take any interest in the objective study of religions. A portion, at least, of this public tries to satisfy its legitimate curiosity by reading very bad books—on the mysteries of the Pyramids, the miracles of Yoga, on the "primordial revelations", or Atlantis—in short, interests itself in the frightful literature of the dilettanti, the neo-spiritualists or pseudo-occultists.

To some degree, it is we, the historians of religions, who are responsible for this. We wanted at all costs to present an *objective* history of religions, but we failed to bear in mind that what we were christening *objectivity* followed the fashion of thinking in our times. For nearly a century we have been striving to set up the history of religions as an autonomous discipline, without success: the history of religions is still, as we all know, confused with anthropology, ethnology, sociology, religious psychology and even with orientalism. Desirous to achieve by all means the prestige of a "science", the history of religions has passed through all the crises of the modern scientific mind, one after another. Historians of religions have been successively—and some of them have not ceased to be—positivists, empiricists, rationalists or historicists. And what is more, none of the fashions which in succession have dominated this study of ours, not one of the global systems put forward in explanation of the religious phenomenon, has been the work of a historian of religions; they have all derived from hypotheses advanced by eminent linguists, anthropologists, sociologists or ethnologists, and have been accepted in their turn by everyone, including the historians of religions!

The situation that one finds today is as follows: a considerable improvement in information, paid for by excessive specialisation and even by sacrificing our own vocation (for the majority of historians of religions have become orientalists, classicists, ethnologists, etc.), and a dependence upon the methods elaborated by modern historiography or sociology (as though the historical study of a ritual or a myth were exactly the same thing as that of a country or of some primitive people). In short, we have neglected this essential fact: that in the title of the "history of religions" the accent ought not to be upon the word *history*, but upon the word *religions*. For although there are numerous ways of practising *history*—from the history of technics to that of human thought—there is only one way of approaching *religion*—namely, to deal with the religious facts. Before making the *history* of anything, one must have a proper understanding of what it *is*, in and for itself. In that connection, I would draw attention to the work of Professor Van der Leeuw, who has done so much for the phenomenology of religion, and whose many and brilliant publications have aroused the educated public to a renewal of interest in the history of religions in general.

In an indirect way, the same interest has been awakened by the discoveries of psychoanalysis and depth-psychology, in the first place by the work of Professor Jung. Indeed, it was soon recognised that the enormous domain of the history of religions provided an inexhaustible supply of terms of comparison with the behaviour of the individual or the collective psyche, as this was studied by psychologists or analysts. As we all know, the use that

psychologists have made of such socio-religious documentation
has not always obtained the approval of historians of religions.
We shall be examining, in a moment, the objections raised against
such comparisons, and indeed they have often been too daring.
But it may be said at once that if the historians of religions had
only approached the objects of their study from a more spiritual
standpoint, if they had tried to gain a deeper insight into archaic
religious symbolisms, many psychological or psychoanalytic interpretations, which look all too flimsy to a specialist's eye, would
never have been suggested. The psychologists have found excellent materials in our books, but very few explanations of any
depth—and they have been tempted to fill up these lacunae by
taking over the work of the historians of religions by putting
forward general—and too often rash—hypotheses.

In few words, the difficulties that have to be overcome today
are these: (a) on the one hand, having decided to compete for the
prestige of an objective "scientific" historiography, the history of
religions is obliged to face the objections that can be raised
against historicism as such; and (b) on the other hand, it is also
obliged to take up the challenge lately presented to it by psychology in general—and particularly by depth-psychology, which,
now that it is beginning to work directly upon the historico-
religious data, is putting forward working hypotheses more
promising, more productive, or at any rate more sensational, than
those that are current among historians of religion.

To understand these difficulties better, let us come now to the
subject of the present study: the symbolism of the "Centre". A
historian of religions has the right to ask us: What do you mean
by these terms? What symbols are in question? Among which
peoples and in what cultures? And he might add: You are not
unaware that the epoch of Tylor, of Mannhardt and Frazer is over
and done with; it is no longer allowable today to speak of myths
and rites "in general", or of a uniformity in primitive man's re-
actions to Nature. Those generalisations are abstractions, like
those of "primitive man" in general. What is concrete is the

religious phenomenon manifested in history and through history. And, from the simple fact that it is manifested in history, it is limited, it is conditioned by history. What meaning, then, for the history of religions could there be in such a formula as, for instance, the ritual approach to immortality? We must first specify what kind of immortality is in question; for we cannot be sure, *a priori*, that humanity as a whole has had, spontaneously, the intuition of immortality or even the desire for it. You speak of the "symbolism of the Centre"—what right have you, as a historian of religions, to do so? Can one so lightly generalise? One ought rather to begin by asking oneself: in which culture, and following upon what historical events, did the religious notion of the "Centre", or that of immortality become crystallised? How are these notions integrated and justified, in the organic system of such and such a culture? How are they distributed, and among which peoples? Only after having answered all these preliminary questions will one have the right to generalise and systematise, to speak in general about the rites of immortality or symbols of the "Centre". If not, one may be contributing to psychology or philosophy, or even theology, but not to the history of religions.

I think all these objections are justified and, inasmuch as I am a historian of religions, I intend to take them into account. But I do not regard them as insurmountable. I know well enough that we are dealing here with religious phenomena and that, by the very fact that they *are* phenomena—that is, manifested or revealed to us—each one is struck, like a medal, by the historical moment in which it was born. There is no "purely" religious fact, outside history and outside time. The noblest religious message, the most universal of mystical experiences, the most universally human behaviour—such, for instance, as religious fear, or ritual, or prayer—is singularised and delimited as soon as it manifests itself. When the Son of God incarnated and became the Christ, he had to speak Aramaic; he could only conduct himself as a Hebrew of his times—and not as a yogi, a Taoist or a shaman. His religious message, however universal it might be, was conditioned by the past and present history of the Hebrew people. If the Son of God had been born in India, his spoken message would have had to conform itself to the structure of the Indian languages, and to the historic and prehistoric tradition of that mixture of peoples.

In the taking up of this position one can clearly recognise the speculative progress that has been made, from Kant—who may be regarded as a precursor of historicism—down to the latest historicist or existentialist philosophers. In so far as man is a historic, concrete, authentic being, he is "in situation". His authentic existence is realising itself in history, in time, in *his* time —which is not that of his father. Neither is it the time of his contemporaries in another continent, or even in another country. That being so, what business have we to be talking about the behaviour of man in general? This man in general is no more than an abstraction: he exists only on the strength of a misunderstanding due to the imperfection of language.

This is not the place to attempt a philosophical critique of historicism and historicist existentialism. That critique has been made, and by more competent authors. Let us remark, for the present, that the view of human spiritual life as historically conditioned resumes, upon another plane and using other dialectical methods, the now somewhat outmoded theories of environmental determinism, geographical, economic, social and even physiological. Everyone agrees that a spiritual fact, being a *human* fact, is necessarily conditioned by everything that works together to make a man, from his anatomy and physiology to language itself. In other words, a spiritual fact presupposes the whole human being —that is, the social man, the economic man, and so forth. But all these conditioning factors together do not, of themselves, add up to the life of the spirit.

What distinguishes the historian of religions from the historian *as such* is that he is dealing with facts which, although historical, reveal a behaviour that goes far beyond the historical involvements of the human being. Although it is true that man is always

found "in situation", his situation is not, for all that, always a
historical one in the sense of being conditioned solely by the contemporaneous historical moment. The man in his totality is aware
of other situations over and above his historical condition; for
example, he knows the state of dreaming, or of the waking dream,
or of melancholy, or of detachment, or of æsthetic bliss, or of
escape, etc.—and none of these states is historical, although they
are as authentic and as important for human existence as man's
historical existence is. Man is also aware of several temporal
rhythms, and not only of historical time—his own time, his
historical contemporaneity. He has only to listen to good music,
to fall in love, or to pray, and he is out of the historical present, he
re-enters the eternal present of love and of religion. Even to open
a novel, or attend a dramatic performance, may be enough to
transport a man into another rhythm of time—what one might
call "condensed time"—which is anyhow not historical time. It
has been too lightly assumed that the authenticity of an existence
depends solely upon the consciousness of its own historicity.
Such historic awareness plays a relatively minor part in human
consciousness, to say nothing of the zones of the unconscious
which also belong to the make-up of the whole human being.
The more a consciousness is awakened, the more it transcends its
own historicity: we have only to remind ourselves of the mystics
and sages of all times, and primarily those of the Orient.

HISTORY AND ARCHETYPES

But let us leave aside the objections that can be raised against
historicism and existentialism, and come back to our problem—
that is, to the dilemmas that confront the historian of religions.
As we were saying, he too often forgets that he is concerned with
archaic and integral human behaviour, and that his business ought
not therefore to be reduced to *recording the historical manifestations
of that behaviour*; he ought also to be trying to gain deeper insight
into its *meanings* and its articulation. To take one example: it is

now known that certain myths and symbols have circulated throughout the world, spread by certain types of culture: this means that those myths and symbols are not, as such, spontaneous discoveries of archaic man, but creations of a well defined cultural complex, elaborated and carried on in certain human societies: such creations have been diffused very far from their original home and have been assimilated by peoples who would not otherwise have known them.

I believe that, after studying as rigorously as possible the relations between certain religious complexes and certain forms of culture, and after verifying the stages of diffusion of these complexes, the *ethnologist* has a right to declare himself satisfied with the results of his researches. But this is not at all the case with the *historian of religions*; for when once the findings of ethnology have been accepted and integrated, the latter has still further problems to raise: for instance, why was it possible for such a myth or such a symbol to become diffused? What did it reveal? Why are certain details—often very important ones—lost during diffusion, whilst others always survive? To sum it up—*what is it that these myths and symbols answer to, that they should have had such a wide diffusion?* These questions cannot be passed over to the psychologists, the sociologists or the philosophers, for none of these are better prepared to resolve them than is the historian of religions.

One has only to take the trouble to study the problem, to find out that, whether obtained by diffusion or spontaneously discovered, myths and rites always disclose a *boundary situation* of man—not only a historical situation. A boundary situation is one which man discovers in becoming conscious of his place in the universe. It is primarily by throwing light upon these boundary situations that the historian of religions fulfils his task and assists in the researches of depth-psychology and even philosophy. This study is possible; moreover, it has already begun. By directing attention to the survival of symbols and mythical themes in the psyche of modern man, by showing that the spontaneous rediscovery of the archetypes of archaic symbolism is a common occurrence in all human beings, irrespective of race and historical surroundings, depth-psychology has freed the historian of religions from his last hesitations. We will give a few examples, in a moment, of this spontaneous rediscovery of archaic symbolism, and we shall see what these can teach a historian of religions.

But already one can guess what perspectives would open up before the history of religions if only it knew how to profit by all its discoveries together with those of ethnology, sociology and depth-psychology. By envisaging the study of man not only inasmuch as he is a historic being, but also as a living symbol, the history of religions could become (if we may be pardoned the word) a *metapsychoanalysis*. For this would lead to an awakening, and a renewal of consciousness, of the archaic symbols and archetypes, whether still living or now fossilised in the religious traditions of all mankind. We have dared to use the term metapsychoanalysis because what is in question here is a more spiritual technique, applicable mainly to elucidating the theoretical content of the symbols and archetypes, giving transparency and coherence to what is allusive, cryptic or fragmentary. One could equally well call this a new *maieutics*. Just as Socrates, according to the *Theaetetus* (149 a, 161 e), acted on the mind obstetrically, bringing to birth thoughts it did not know it contained, so the history of religions could bring forth a new man, more authentic and more complete: for, through the study of the religious traditions, modern man would not only rediscover a kind of archaic behaviour, he would also become conscious of the spiritual riches implied in such behaviour.

This maieutics effected with the aid of religious symbolism would also help to rescue modern man from his cultural provincialism and, above all, from his historical and existentialist relativism. For, as we shall see, man is opposing himself to history even when he sets out to make history, and even when he pretends to be nothing but "history". And in so far as man surpasses his historic moment and gives free course to his desire to relive the archetypes, he realises himself as a whole and universal being. In so far as he opposes himself to history, modern man rediscovers the archetypal positions. Even his sleep, even his orgiastic tendencies are charged with spiritual significance. By the simple fact that, at the heart of his being, he rediscovers the cosmic rhythms —the alternations of day and night, for instance, or of winter and summer—he comes to a more complete knowledge of his own destiny and significance.

Still with the aid of the history of religions, man might recover the symbolism of his body, which is an anthropocosmos. What the various techniques of the imagination, and especially the poetic techniques, have realised in this direction is almost nothing beside what the history of religions might promise. All these things still exist even in modern man; it is only necessary to reactivate them and bring them to the level of consciousness. By regaining awareness of his own anthropocosmic symbolism— which is only one variety of the archaic symbolism—modern man will obtain a new existential dimension, totally unknown to present-day existentialism and historicism: this is an authentic and major mode of being, which defends man from nihilism and historical relativism without thereby taking him out of history. For history itself will one day be able to find its true meaning: that of the epiphany of a glorious and absolute human condition. We have only to recall the value attached to historical existence by Judæo-Christianity, to realise how, and in what sense, history might become "glorious" and even "absolute".

Obviously, one could never pretend that rational study of the history of religions should, or could, be substituted for religious experience itself, still less for the experience of faith. But even for the Christian consciousness, a maieutics effected by means of the archaic symbolism will bear its fruit. Christianity is the inheritor of a very ancient and very complex religious tradition whose structures have survived in the midst of the Church, even though the spiritual values and theological orientation have changed. And in any case, nothing whatever, throughout the Cosmos, that is a manifestation of glory—to speak in Christian terms—can be a matter of indifference to a believer.

Finally, the study of religions will shed light upon one fact that until now has been insufficiently noted, namely, that there is a logic of the symbol. Certain groups of symbols, at least, prove to be coherent, logically connected with one another;[1] in a word, they can be systematically formulated, translated into rational terms. This internal logic of symbols raises a problem with far-reaching consequences: are certain zones of the individual or collective consciousness dominated by the *logos*, or are we concerned here with manifestations of a "transconscious"? That problem cannot be resolved by depth-psychology alone, for the symbolisms which decipher the latter are for the most part made up of scattered fragments and of the manifestations of a psyche in crisis, if not in a state of pathological regression. To grasp the authentic structures and functions of symbols, one must turn to the inexhaustible indices of the history of religions; and yet even here, one must know how to choose; for our documents are in many cases decadent in form, aberrant, or frankly second-rate. If we want to arrive at an adequate understanding of archaic religious symbolism we are obliged to make a selection, just as, in order to gain some idea of a foreign literature, we must not take at hazard the first ten or the first hundred books to be found in the nearest public library. It is to be hoped that one day the historians of religion will make a hierarchic assessment of their documents according to the value and the condition of each, as do their colleagues, the historians of literature. But here again, we are only at the beginning of things.

THE IMAGE OF THE WORLD

In archaic and traditional societies, the surrounding world is conceived as a microcosm. At the limits of this closed world begins the domain of the unknown, of the formless. On this side

[1]See below, in Chapter III, *the "god who binds", and the symbolism of knots.*

there is ordered—because inhabited and organised—space; on the other, outside this familiar space, there is the unknown and dangerous region of the demons, the ghosts, the dead and of foreigners—in a word, chaos or death or night. This image of an inhabited microcosm, surrounded by desert regions regarded as a chaos or a kingdom of the dead, has survived even in highly evolved civilisations such as those of China, Mesopotamia and Egypt. Indeed, a good many texts liken the enemies who are attacking national territory to ghosts, demons or the powers of chaos. Thus the adversaries of the Pharaoh were looked upon as "sons of ruin, wolves, dogs", etc. The Pharaoh was likened to the God Rē, victor over the dragon Apophis, whilst his enemies were identified with that same mythical dragon. Because they attack, and endanger the equilibrium and the very life of the city (or of any other inhabited and organised territory), enemies are assimilated to demonic powers, trying to reincorporate the microcosm into the state of chaos; that is, to suppress it. The destruction of an established order, the abolition of an archetypal image, was equivalent to a regression into chaos, into the pre-formal, undifferentiated state that preceded the cosmogony. Let us note that the same images are still invoked in our own days when people want to formulate the dangers that menace a certain type of civilisation: there is much talk of "chaos", of "disorder", of the "dark ages" into which "our world" is subsiding. All these expressions, it is felt, signify the abolition of an order, of a Cosmos, of a structure, and the re-immersion in a state that is fluid, amorphous, in the end chaotic.

The conception of the enemy as a demonic being, a veritable incarnation of the powers of evil, has also survived until our days. The psychoanalysis of these mythic images that still animate the modern world will perhaps show us the extent to which we project our own destructive desires upon the "enemy". But that is a problem beyond our competence. What we wish to bring to

See our book *The Myth of the Eternal Return*, New York-London, 1954, pp. 37 ff.

light is that, for the archaic world in general, the enemies threatening the microcosm were dangerous, not in their capacity as human beings but because they were incarnating the hostile and destructive powers. It is very probable that the defences of inhabited areas and cities began by being magical defences; for these defences—ditches, labyrinths, ramparts, etc.—were set up to prevent the incursions of evil spirits rather than attacks from human beings. Even fairly late in history, in the Middle Ages for instance, the walls of cities were ritually consecrated as a defence against the Devil, sickness and death. Moreover, the archaic symbolism finds no difficulty in assimilating the human enemy to the Devil or to Death. After all, the result of their attacks, whether demonic or military, is always the same: ruin, disintegration and death.

Every microcosm, every inhabited region, has what may be called a "Centre"; that is to say, a place that is sacred above all. It is there, in that Centre, that the sacred manifests itself in its totality, either in the form of elementary hierophanies—as it does among the "primitives" (in the totemic centres, for example, the caves where the *tchuringas* are buried, etc.)—or else in the more evolved form of the direct epiphanies of the gods, as in the traditional civilisations. But we must not envisage this symbolism of the Centre with the geometrical implications that it has to a Western scientific mind. For each one of these microcosms there may be several "centres". As we shall see before long, all the Oriental civilisations—Mesopotamia, India, China, etc.—recognised an unlimited number of "Centres". Moreover, each one of these "Centres" was considered and even literally called the "Centre of the World". The place in question being a "sacred space", consecrated by a hierophany, or ritually constructed, and not a profane, homogeneous, geometrical space, the plurality of "Centres of the Earth" within a single inhabited region presented no difficulty.[3] What we have here is a sacred, mythic geography, the only kind effectually *real*, as opposed to profane geography,

[3] See our *Patterns in Comparative Religion*, London, 1958, pp. 367 ff.

the latter being "objective" and, as it were, abstract and non-essential—the theoretical construction of a space and a world that we do not live in, and therefore do not *know*.

In mythical geography, sacred space is the essentially *real space*, for, as it has lately been shown, in the archaic world the myth alone is real. It tells of manifestations of the only indubitable reality—the *sacred*. It is in such space that one has direct contact with the sacred—whether this be materialised in certain objects (*tchuringas*, representations of the divinity, etc.) or manifested in the hiero-cosmic symbols (the Pillar of the World, the Cosmic Tree, etc.). In cultures that have the conception of three cosmic regions—those of Heaven, Earth and Hell—the "centre" constitutes the point of intersection of those regions. It is here that the break-through on to another plane is possible and, at the same time, communication between the three regions. We have reason to believe that this image of three cosmic levels is quite archaic; we meet with it, for instance, among the Semang pygmies of the Malay peninsula: at the centre of their world there stands an enormous rock, Batu-Ribn, and beneath it is Hell. From the Batu-Ribn a tree-trunk formerly reached up towards the sky.[4] Hell, the centre of the earth and the "door" of heaven are all to be found, then, upon the same axis, and it is along this axis that the passage from one cosmic region to another is effected. We might hesitate to believe in the authenticity of this cosmological theory among the Semang pygmies, were we not bound to admit that the same theory already existed in outline in prehistoric times.[5] The Semang say that the trunk of a tree *formerly* connected the summit of the Cosmic Mountain, the Centre of the World, with Heaven. This is an allusion to a mythic theme of extremely wide diffusion: formerly, communication with Heaven and relations with the divinity were easy and "natural"; until, in con-

[4] P. Schebesta, *Les Pygmées* (French translation), Paris, 1940, pp. 156 ff.

[5] Cf., for example, W. Gaerte, "Kosmische Vorstellungen im Bilde prähistorischer Zeit: Erdberg, Himmelsberg, Erdnabel und Weltenströme" in *Anthropos* IX, 1914, pp. 956-979.

sequence of a ritual fault, these communications were broken off, and the gods withdrew to still higher heavens. Only medicine-men, shamans, priests, and heroes, or the sovereign rulers were now able to re-establish communication with Heaven, and that only in a temporary way and for their own use.[6] The myth of a primordial paradise, lost on account of some fault or other, is of extreme importance—but although in some ways it touches upon our subject, we cannot discuss it now.

SYMBOLISM OF THE "CENTRE"

Let us now return to the image of the three cosmic regions connected in a "Centre" along one axis. It is chiefly in the early Oriental civilisations that we meet with this archetypal image. The name of the sanctuaries of Nippur, Larsa and Sippara was *Dur-an-ki*, "link between Heaven and Earth". Babylon had a whole list of names, among others "House of the basis of Heaven and Earth" and "Link between Heaven and Earth". But there was also in Babylon the link between the Earth and the lower regions, for the town had been built upon *bāb-apsū*, the "Gate of *apsū*"; *apsū* meaning the waters of Chaos before the Creation. We find the same tradition among the Hebrews. The Rock of Jerusalem went deep down into the subterranean waters (*tehōm*). It is said in the Mishna that the Temple stood just over the *tehōm* (the Hebrew equivalent for *apsū*). And just as, in Babylon, they had "the Gate of *apsū*", so in Jerusalem the Rock of the Temple covered the "mouth of the *tehōm*". We encounter similar traditions in the Indo-European world. Among the Romans, for example, the *mundus* constitutes the meeting-point between the lower regions and the terrestrial world. The Italic temple was the zone of inter-section between the higher (divine) world, the terrestrial world and the subterranean (infernal) world.[7]

Every Oriental city was standing, in effect, at the centre of the

[6] Cf. our *Le Chamanisme et les techniques de l'extase*, Payot, 1951.
[7] Cf. *The Myth of the Eternal Return*, pp. 13 ff.

world. Babylon was *Bāb-ilānī*, a "gate of the Gods", for it was there that the gods came down to earth. The capital of the ideal Chinese sovereign was situated near to the miraculous Tree "shaped Wood" (*Kien-mou*) at the intersection of the three cosmic zones, Heaven, Earth and Hell. Examples could be multiplied without end. These cities, temples or palaces, regarded as Centres of the World are all only replicas, repeating *ad libitum* the same archaic image—the Cosmic Mountain, the World Tree or the central Pillar which sustains the planes of the Cosmos.

This symbol of a Mountain, a Tree or a Column situated at the Centre of the World is extremely widely distributed. We may recall the Mount Meru of Indian tradition, Haraberezaiti of the Iranians, the Norse Himingbjör, the "Mount of the Lands" in the Mesopotamian tradition, Mount Tabor in Palestine (which may signify *tabbur*—that is, "navel" or *omphalos*), Mount Gerizim, again in Palestine, which is expressly named the "navel of the earth", and Golgotha which, for Christians, represented the centre of the world, etc.[8] Because the territory, the city, the temple or the royal palace thus stood at the "Centre of the World"— that is, on the summit of the Cosmic Mountain—each was regarded as the highest place in the world, the only one which had not been submerged at the Deluge. "The land of Israel was not submerged by the Deluge," says a rabbinical text. And, according to Islamic tradition, the highest elevated place on earth is the Kā'aba, because "the Pole Star proves that . . . it lies over against the centre of Heaven"[9] The names of sacred Babylonian towers and temples show that they were assimilated to the Cosmic Mountain; that is, to the Centre of the World—"Mount of the House", "House of the Mountain of all the lands", "Mount of Storms", "Bond between Heaven and Earth", etc. The *ziqqurat* was, properly speaking, a cosmic mountain—that is, a symbolic image of the Cosmos; its seven stages represented the seven planetary spheres; by ascending them, the priest attained to the

[8] Cf. *Patterns in Comparative Religion*, pp. 374 ff.
[9] For the texts, see our *Myth of the Eternal Return*, pp. 13 ff.

summit of the Universe. This same symbolism informs the colossal construction of the temple of Barabudur, which is shaped like an artificial mountain. To ascend it is equivalent to an ecstatic journey to the Centre of the World; upon reaching the highest terrace, the pilgrim experiences the break-through into another state; he transcends profane space and enters into a "pure region". Here we are in the presence of a "rite of the centre."[10]

The summit of the Cosmic Mountain is not only the highest point on the Earth, it is the navel of the Earth, the point at which creation began. "The Holy One created the world like an embryo," affirms a rabbinical text. "As an embryo proceeds from the navel onward, so God began the creation of the world from its navel onward, and from thence it spread in different directions." "The world was created, beginning at Sion," says another text. The same symbolism occurs in Ancient India, in the *Rig Veda*; where the Universe is conceived as expanding outward from a central point.[11]

The creation of man, a replica of the cosmogony, took place similarly from a central point, in the Centre of the World. According to the Mesopotamian tradition, man was fashioned at the "navel of the earth", where there is also *Dur-an-ki*, the "link between Heaven and Earth". Ohrmazd created the primordial man Gajomard, at the centre of the world. The Paradise in which Adam was created out of clay is, of course, situated at the Centre of the Cosmos. Paradise was the "navel of the Earth" and, according to a Syrian tradition, was established "upon a mountain higher than all the others". According to the Syrian book *The Cavern of Treasures*, Adam was created at the centre of the earth, on the very same spot where, later on, the Cross of Jesus was to be erected. The same traditions have been preserved by Judaism. The Judaic apocalypse and the *Midrash* specify that Adam was fashioned in Jerusalem. And Adam, having been buried at the

[10] For the texts, see our *Patterns in Comparative Religion*, pp. 376 ff.

[11] *Patterns in Comparative Religion*, p. 377; *The Myth of the Eternal Return*, p. 16.

same spot where he was created—that is, at the centre of the world, upon Golgotha—the blood of the Lord will redeem him also.[12]

The most widely distributed variant of the symbolism of the Centre is the Cosmic Tree, situated in the middle of the Universe, and upholding the three worlds as upon one axis. Vedic India, ancient China and the Germanic mythology, as well as the "primitive" religions, all held different versions of this Cosmic Tree, whose roots plunged down into Hell, and whose branches reached to Heaven. In the Central and North Asiatic mythologies its seven or nine branches symbolise the seven or nine celestial planes—that is, the seven planetary heavens. We have not room here to enlarge upon the complex symbolism of this Tree of the World;[13] what concerns us now is the part it plays in the "rites of the centre". It may be said, in general, that the majority of the sacred and ritual trees that we meet with in the history of religions are only replicas, imperfect copies of this exemplary archetype, the Cosmic Tree. Thus, all these sacred trees are thought of as situated in the Centre of the World, and all the ritual trees or posts which are consecrated before or during any religious ceremony are, as it were, magically projected into the Centre of the World. Let us content ourselves with a few examples

In Vedic India, the sacrificial stake (*yūpa*) is made of a tree which is similar to the Universal Tree. While it is being felled, the priest of the sacrifice addresses these words to it: "With thy summit, do not rend the Heavens; with thy trunk, wound not the atmosphere . . ." It is easy to see that what we have here is the Cosmic Tree itself. From the wood of this tree the sacrificial stake is fashioned, and this becomes a sort of cosmic pillar: "Lift thyself up, O Lord of the forest, unto the summit of the earth!" is the invocation of the *Rig Veda* (III, 8, 3). "With thy summit

[12] *Patterns in Comparative Religion*, p. 378.
[13] Cf. our *Patterns in Comparative Religion*, pp. 269 ff.; *Le Chamanisme* . . ., pp. 244 ff.; and, upon the Christian symbolism of the Cross as the Cosmic Tree, see H. de Lubac, *Aspects du Bouddhisme*, Paris 1951, pp. 61 ff.

thou dost hold up the Heavens, with thy branches thou fillest the air, with thy foot thou steadiest the earth," proclaims the *Satapatha Brāhmana* (III, 7, 1, 4).

The installation and consecration of the sacrificial stake constitute a rite of the Centre. Assimilated to the Cosmic Tree, the stake becomes in its turn the axis connecting the three cosmic regions. Communication between Heaven and Earth becomes possible by means of this pillar. He who makes the sacrifice does, indeed, go up to heaven, alone or with his wife, upon this post now ritually transformed into the World-Axis itself. While setting up the ladder, he says to his wife: "Come, let us go up to Heaven!" She answers: "Let us go up!" (*Sat. Br.* V, 2, 1, 9), and they begin to mount the ladder. At the top, while touching the head of the post, the sacrificer cries out: "We have reached Heaven!" (*Taittirīya Samhitā, Sat. Br.*, etc.) Or, while climbing up the steps of the stake, he stretches out his arms (as a bird spreads its wings!) and on reaching the top cries out: "I have attained to heaven, to the gods: I have become immortal!" (*Taittirīya Samhitā*, 1, 7, 9.) "In truth," continues the *Taittirīya Samhitā* (VI, 6, 4, 2), "the sacrificer makes himself a ladder and a bridge to reach the celestial world."

The bridge or ladder between Heaven and Earth were possible because they were set up in a Centre of the World—like the ladder seen in a dream by Jacob, which reached from earth to the heavens. "And behold! the angels of God were ascending and descending on it" (*Genesis* XXVIII, 11-12). The Indian rite also alludes to the immortality that is attained in consequence of the ascent into Heaven. As we shall see presently, a number of other ritual approaches to a Centre are equivalent to a conquest of immortality.

The assimilation of the ritual tree to the Cosmic Tree is still more apparent in Central and North Asiatic shamanism. The climbing of such a tree by the Tatar shaman symbolises his ascension to heaven. In fact, seven or nine notches are cut in the tree and the shaman, while he is climbing up them, makes the pertinent declaration that he is going up to heaven: he describes to the onlookers all that he sees at each of the celestial levels which he passes through. At the sixth heaven he worships the moon, at the seventh, the sun. Finally, at the ninth, he prostrates himself before Bai Ulgän, the Supreme Being, and offers him the soul of the horse that has been sacrificed.[14]

The shamanic tree is only a replica of the Tree of the World, which rises in the middle of the Universe and at whose summit is the supreme God, or the solarised god. The seven or nine notches on the shamanic tree symbolise the seven or nine branches of the Cosmic Tree—that is, the seven or nine heavens. The shaman feels, moreover, that he is united with this Tree of the World through other mystical relationships. In his initiatory dreams, the future shaman is believed to approach the Cosmic Tree and to receive, from the hand of God himself, three branches of it, which are to serve as frames for his drums.[15] We know the indispensable part that is played by the drum during the shamanic ceremonies; it is above all by the aid of their drums that shamans attain to the ecstatic state. And, when we think that *the drum is made of the very wood of the World Tree*, we can understand the symbolism and the religious value of the sounds of the shamanic drum—and why, when he beats it, the shaman feels himself transported in ecstasy near to the Tree of the World.[16] Here we have a mystical journey to the "Centre", and thence into the highest heaven. Thus, either by climbing up the seven or nine notches of the ceremonial birch-tree, or simply drumming, the shaman sets out on his journey to heaven, but he can only obtain that rupture of the cosmic planes which makes his ascension possible or enables him to fly ecstatic-ally through the heavens, because he is thought to be already at

[14] Cf. the material and the bibliography in our book *Le Chamanisme*, pp. 171 ff.
[15] A. A. Popov, *Tavgijcy. Materialy po etnografii avamskich i vedeevskich tavgicev* (Moscow-Leningrad 1936), pp. 84 ff. See also *Le Chamanisme et les techniques archaïques de l'extase*, pp. 160 ff.
[16] Cf. E. Emsheimer, "Schamanentrommel und Trommelbaum" in *Ethnos*, Vol. IV, 1946, pp. 166-181.

the very Centre of the world; for, as we have seen, it is only in such a Centre that communication between Earth, Heaven and Hell is possible.[17]

SYMBOLISM OF ASCENSION

It is highly probable, at least in the case of the Central Asiatic and Siberian religions, that this symbolism of the Centre was influenced by some Indo-Iranian and, in the last analysis, Mesopotamian cosmological systems. The importance of the number seven seems, among other things, to prove this. But it is important to distinguish between the borrowing of a cosmological theory elaborated *around* the symbolism of the Centre—such as, for example, the conception of the seven celestial spheres—and the symbolism of the Centre *in itself*. We have already seen that this symbolism is extremely archaic, that it is known to the pygmies of the Malay Peninsula. And even if we might suspect a remote Indian influence among these Semang pygmies, we should still have to explain the symbolism of the Centre that is found upon the prehistoric monuments (cosmic mountains, the four rivers, the Tree, the spiral, etc.). Furthermore, it has been possible to show that the symbolism of a cosmic axis was already known in the archaic cultures (the *Urkulturen* of the Graebner-Schmidt school) especially among the Arctic and North American populations; the centre-post of the cabin they live in is assimilated to the Cosmic Axis. And it is at the foot of this post that one deposits the offerings intended for the heavenly divinities, for it is only along this axis that offerings can mount up into heaven.[18] When the form of the dwelling is changed and the hut is replaced by the yourt (as, for example, among the nomadic stock-breeders of central Asia), the mythico-ritual function of the central pillar is

[17] The initiatory ascent of a ceremonial tree is also met with in Indonesian, South American (Araucan) and North American (Pomo) shamanism. Cf. *Le Chamanisme . . .*, pp. 122 ff., 125 ff.

[18] See *Le Chamanisme . . .*, pp. 235 ff.

performed through the opening left in the roof to let out the smoke. On sacrificial occasions, they bring a tree into the yourt, so that the top of it projects through this opening. This sacrificial tree with its seven branches symbolises the seven celestial spheres. Thus, on the one hand, *the house is made to symbolise the universe* and, on the other, *is supposed to be situated in the Centre of the World*, the smoke-hole opening upwards towards the Pole Star.

We shall return presently to this symbolic assimilation of the dwelling-place to the "Centre of the World", for it expresses one of the most instructive customs of archaic religious man. For the moment, let us look at the ritual of ascension that takes place in a "centre". We saw that the Tatar or Siberian shaman climbs a tree, and that the Vedic sacrificer mounts a ladder: the two rites are directed to the same end, the ascension into Heaven. A good many of the myths speak of a tree, of a creeper, a cord, or a thread of spider-web or a ladder which connects Earth with Heaven, and by means of which certain privileged beings do, in effect, mount up to heaven. These myths have, of course, their ritual correlatives— as, for instance, the shamanic tree or the post in the Vedic sacrifice. The ceremonial staircase plays an equally important part, of which we will now give a few examples:

Polyaenus (*Stratagematon*, VII, 22) tells us of Kosingas, the priest-king of certain peoples of Thrace, who threatened to desert his subjects by going up a wooden ladder to the goddess Hera; which proves that such a ritual ladder existed and was believed to be a means whereby the priest-king could ascend to Heaven. The ascension to Heaven by ritually climbing up a ladder was probably part of an Orphic initiation; in any case, we find it again in the Mithraic initiation. In the mysteries of Mithra the ceremonial ladder (*climax*) had seven rungs, each being made of a different metal. According to Celsus (Origen, *Contra Celsum*, VI, 22), the first rung was made of lead, corresponding to the "heaven" of the planet Saturn; the second of tin (Venus); the third of bronze (Jupiter); the fourth of iron (Mercury); the fifth of "monetary alloy" (Mars); the sixth of silver (the Moon) and the seventh of gold (the Sun). The eighth rung, Celsus tells us, represented the sphere of the fixed stars.[19] By going up this ceremonial ladder, the initiate was supposed to pass through the seven heavens, thus uplifting himself even to the Empyrean—just as one attained to the ultimate heaven by ascending the seven stages of the Babylonian *ziqqurat*, or as one travelled through the different cosmic regions by scaling the terraces of the Temple of Barabudur, which in itself, as we saw, constituted a Cosmic Mountain and an *imago mundi*.

We can easily understand that the stairway in the Mithraic initiation was an Axis of the World and was situated at the Centre of the Universe: otherwise the rupture of the planes would not have been possible. "Initiation" means, as we know, the symbolic death and resurrection of the neophyte or, in other contexts, the descent into Hell followed by ascension into Heaven. Death—whether initiatory or not—is the supreme case of a rupture of the planes. That is why it is symbolised by a climbing of steps, and why funerary rites often make use of ladders or stairways. The soul of the deceased ascends the pathways up a mountain, or climbs a tree or a creeper, right up into the heavens. We meet with something of this conception all over the world, from ancient Egypt to Australia. In Assyrian, the common expression for the verb "to die" is "to clutch the mountain". Similarly in Egyptian, *myny*, "to clutch" is a euphemism for "to die". In the Indian mythological tradition, Yama, the first man to die, climbed up the mountain and over "the high passes" in order to show "the path to many" as it is said in the *Rig Veda* (X, 14, 1). The road of the dead, in popular Ural-Altaic beliefs, leads up the mountains: Bolot, the Kara-Kirghiz hero and also Kesar, legendary king of the Mongols, enter into the world of the beyond by way of an initiatory ordeal, through a cave at the summit of the mountains: the descent of the

[19] Cf. the materials brought together in our *Le Chamanisme*, pp. 248 ff. For the Christian symbolism of ascension, see Louis Beirnaert, " Le Symbolisme ascensionnel dans la liturgie et la mystique chrétiennes" in the *Eranos Jahrbuch*, XIX, Zürich, 1951, pp. 41-63.

shaman into Hell is also effected by way of a cavern. The Egyptians have preserved, in their funerary texts, the expression *asket
pet* (*asket* means "a step") to indicate that the ladder at the disposal of Rē is a real ladder, linking Earth to Heaven. "The ladder
is set up that I may see the gods," says the *Book of the Dead*, and
again, "the gods make him a ladder, so that, by making use of it,
he may go up to Heaven." In many tombs of the periods of the
archaic and the middle dynastics, amulets have been found en-
graved with a ladder (*maqet*) or a staircase. The custom of the
funerary ladder has, moreover, survived until our days: several
primitive Asian peoples—as, for instance, the Lolos, the
Karens and others—set up ritual ladders upon tombs, to enable
the deceased to ascend to heaven.[20]

As we have just seen, the ladder can carry an extremely rich
symbolism without ceasing to be perfectly coherent. *It gives
plastic expression to the break through the planes necessitated by the
passage from one mode of being to another*, by placing us at the cosmological point *where communication between Heaven, Earth and Hell
becomes possible*. That is why the stairway and the ladder play so
considerable a part in the rites and the myths of initiation, as well
as in funerary rituals, not to mention the rites of royal or sacer-
dotal enthronement or those of marriage. But we also know that
the symbolism of climbing-up and of stairs recurs often enough in
psychoanalytic literature, an indication that it belongs to the
archaic content of the human psyche and is not a "historical"
creation, not an innovation dating from a certain historical moment (say, from ancient Egypt or Vedic India, etc.). I will content
myself with a single example of a spontaneous rediscovery of
this primordial symbolism.[21]

Julien Green notes, in his Journal for the 4th of April, 1933,
that "In all my books, the idea of fear or of any other fairly strong
emotion seems linked in some inexplicable manner to a staircase.

[20] See *Patterns in Comparative Religion*, pp. 102 ff. and *Le Chamanisme et les
techniques archaïques de l'extase*, pp. 420 ff.
[21] See our *Myths, Dreams and Mysteries*, London, 1960, pp. 15 ff.

I realised this yesterday, whilst I was passing in review all the novels that I have written . . . (here follow the references). I wonder how I can have so often repeated this effect without noticing it. As a child, I used to dream I was being chased on a staircase. My mother had the same fears in her young days; perhaps something of them has remained with me. . . ."

We now know why the idea of fear, for Julien Green, was associated with the image of a staircase, and why all the dramatic events he described in his works—love, death, or crime—happened upon a staircase. The act of climbing or ascending symbolises *the way towards the absolute reality*; and to the profane consciousness, the approach towards that reality arouses an ambivalent feeling, of fear and of joy, of attraction and repulsion, etc. The ideas of sanctification, of death, love and deliverance are all involved in the symbolism of stairs. Indeed, each of these modes of being represents a cessation of the profane human condition; that is, a breaking of the ontological plane. Through love and death, sanctity and metaphysical knowledge, man passes—as it is said in the *Brihadāranyaka Upanishad*, from the "unreal to the reality".

But it must not be forgotten that the staircase symbolises these things because it is thought to be set up in a "centre", because it makes communication possible between the different levels of being, and, finally, because it is a concrete formula for the mythical ladder, for the creeper or the spider-web, the Cosmic Tree or the Pillar of the Universe, that connects the three cosmic zones.

CONSTRUCTION OF A "CENTRE"

We have seen that it was not only temples that were thought to be situated at the "Centre of the World", but that every holy place, every place that bore witness to an incursion of the sacred into profane space, was also regarded as a "centre". These sacred spaces could also be constructed; but their construction was, in its

way, a cosmogony—a creation of the world—which is only
natural since, as we have seen, the world was created in the
beginning from an embryo, from a "centre". Thus, for instance,
the construction of the Vedic fire altar reproduced the creation of
the world, and the altar itself was a microcosm, an *imago mundi*.
The water in which one mixes the clay is, as the *Satapatha
Brāhmana* tells us (I, 9, 2, 29; VI, 5, 1, etc.), the primordial Water;
the clay that serves as a base for the altar is the Earth; its lateral
walls represent the atmosphere, etc. (Perhaps it should be added
that this construction also implies a construction of cosmic Time,
but we have not room to go into that problem here.)[22]

It is unnecessary, then, to insist that the history of religions
records a considerable number of ritual constructions of a
"Centre". Let us, however, note one thing which is of importance
in our view: to the degree that the ancient holy places, temples or
altars, lose their religious efficacy, people discover and apply other
geomantic, architectural or iconographic formulas which, in the
end, sometimes astonishingly enough, represent the same symbolism of the "Centre". To give a single example: the construction
of a *mandala*.[23] The term itself means "a circle"; the translations
from the Tibetan sometimes render it by "centre" and sometimes
by "that which surrounds". In fact a *mandala* represents a whole
series of circles, concentric or otherwise, inscribed within a square;
and in this diagram, drawn on the ground by means of coloured
threads or coloured rice powder, the various divinities of the
Tantric pantheon are arranged in order. The *mandala* thus represents an *imago mundi* and at the same time a symbolic pantheon.
The initiation of the neophyte consists, among other things, in
his entering into the different zones and gaining access to the
different levels of the *mandala*. This rite of penetration may be

[22] See *The Myth of the Eternal Return*, pp. 79 ff.
[23] Cf. our *Yoga, Immortality and Freedom*, New York-London, 1958, pp. 219 ff.;
Giuseppe Tucci, *Teoria e pratica del mandala*, Rome, 1949; on the symbolism of
the *mandala*, see C. G. Jung, *Psychology and Alchemy*, London, 1953, pp. 91 ff.;
and the same author's *Gestaltungen des Unbewussten*, Zürich, 1950, pp. 187 ff.

regarded as equivalent to the well-known rite of walking round a
temple (*pradakshina*), or to the progressive elevation, terrace by
terrace, up to the "pure lands" at the highest levels of the temple.
On the other hand, the placing of the neophyte in a *mandala* may
be likened to the initiation by entry into a labyrinth: certain
mandalas have, moreover, a clearly labyrinthine character. The
function of the *mandala* may be considered at least twofold, as is
that of the labyrinth. On the one hand, penetration into a *mandala*
drawn on the ground is equivalent to an initiation ritual; and, on
the other hand, the *mandala* "protects" the neophyte against every
harmful force from without, and at the same time helps him to
concentrate, to find his own "centre".

But every Indian temple, seen from above, is a *mandala*. Any
Indian temple is, like a *mandala*, a microcosm and at the same time
a pantheon. Why, then, need one construct a *mandala*—why did
they want a new "Centre of the World"? Simply because, for
certain devotees, who felt in need of a more authentic and a deeper
religious experience, the traditional ritual had become fossilised:
the construction of a fire altar or the ascent of the terraces of a
temple no longer enabled them to rediscover their "centre".
Unlike archaic man or the man of Vedic times, the Tantric
devotee had need of a *personal experience* to reactivate certain
primordial symbols in his consciousness. That is why, moreover,
some Tantric schools rejected the external *mandala*, and had recourse to interiorised *mandalas*. These could be of two kinds:
first, a purely mental construction, which acted as a "support" for
meditation, or, alternatively, an identification of the *mandala* in
his own body. In the former case the yogi places himself mentally
within the *mandala*, and thereby performs an act of concentration
and, at the same time, of "defence" against distraction and
temptation. The *mandala* "concentrates"; it preserves one from
dispersion, from distraction. The discovery of the *mandala* in his
own body indicates a desire to identify his "mystical body" with
a microcosm. A more detailed analysis of this penetration by
means of yoga techniques, into what might be called the "mystical

body", would take us too far. Suffice it to say that the reactivation of the *chakras*—those "wheels" (or circles) which are regarded as so many points of intersection of the cosmic life and the mental life—is homologous with the initiatory penetration into a *mandala*. The awakening of the Kundalini is equivalent to the breaking of the ontological plane; that is, to the plenary realisation of the symbolism of the "Centre".

As we have seen, the *mandala* can be used in support, either at the same time or successively, of a concrete ritual or an act of spiritual concentration or, again, of a technique of mystical physiology. This multivalency, this applicability to multiple although closely comparable planes, is a characteristic of the symbolism of the Centre in general. This is easily understandable, since every human being tends, even unconsciously, towards the Centre, and towards his own centre, where he can find integral reality—sacredness. This desire, so deeply rooted in man, to find himself at the very heart of the real—at the Centre of the World, the place of communication with Heaven—explains the ubiquitous use of "Centres of the World". We have seen above how the habitation of man was assimilated to the Universe, the hearth or the smoke-hole being homologised with the Centre of the World; so that all houses—like all temples, palaces and cities—are situated at one and the same point, the Centre of the Universe.

But is there not a certain contradiction here? A whole array of myths, symbols and rituals emphasises with one accord *the difficulty of obtaining entry into a centre*; while on the other hand another series of myths and rites lays it down that *this centre is accessible*. For example, pilgrimage to the Holy Places is difficult; but any visit whatever to a church is a pilgrimage. The Cosmic Tree is, on the one hand, inaccessible; but on the other, it may be found in any yourt. The way which leads to the "Centre" is sown with obstacles, and yet every city, every temple, every dwelling-place *is already* at the Centre of the Universe. The sufferings and the "trials" undergone by Ulysses are fabulous; nevertheless any *return to hearth and home* whatever is equivalent to Ulysses' return to Ithaca.

All this seems to show that man *can live only in a sacred space*, in the "Centre". We observe that one group of traditions attests the desire of man to find himself at the Centre *without any effort*, whilst another group insists upon the *difficulty*, and consequently upon the *merit*, of being able to enter into it. We are not here concerned to trace the history of either of these traditions. The fact that the first-mentioned—the "easy" way which allows of the construction of a Centre even in a man's own house—is found nearly everywhere, invites us to regard it as the more significant. It calls attention to something in the human condition that we may call the *nostalgia for Paradise*. By this we mean the desire to *find oneself always and without effort* in the Centre of the World, at the heart of reality; and by a short cut and in a natural manner to transcend the human condition, and to recover the divine condition—as a Christian would say, the condition before the Fall.[24]

We should not like to terminate this study without having recalled one European myth which, though only indirectly concerned with the symbolism and rites of the Centre, combines and integrates them in a still vaster symbolism. We refer to an episode in the legend of Parsifal and the Fisher King,[25] concerning the mysterious malady that paralysed the old King who held the secret of the Graal. It was not he alone who suffered; everything around him was falling into ruins, crumbling away—the palace, the towers and the gardens. Animals no longer bred, trees bore no more fruit, the springs were drying up. Many doctors had tried to cure the Fisher King, all without the least success. The knights were arriving there day and night, each of them asking first of all for news of the King's health. But one knight—poor, unknown

[24] Cf. *Patterns in Comparative Religion*, pp. 380 ff., and *Le Chamanisme*, pp. 417, 428 ff.

[25] *Perceval*, Hucher edition, p. 466; Jessie L. Weston, *From Ritual to Romance*, Cambridge, 1920, pp. 12 ff. The same mythic motif occurs in the cycle of Sir Gawain (Weston, *ibid.*).

and even slightly ridiculous—took the liberty of disregarding ceremony and politeness: his name was Parsifal. Paying no attention to courtly custom, he made straight for the King and, addressing him without any preamble, asked: "Where is the Graal?" In that very instant, everything is transformed: the King rises from his bed of suffering, the rivers and fountains flow once more, vegetation grows again, and the castle is miraculously restored. Those few words of Parsifal had been enough to re-generate the whole of Nature. But those few words propound the central question, the one question that can arouse not only the Fisher King but the whole Cosmos: Where is the supreme reality, the sacred, the Centre of Life and the source of immort-ality, where is the Holy Graal? No one had thought, until then, of asking that central question—and the world was perishing because of that metaphysical and religious indifference, because of lack of imagination and absence of desire for reality.

That brief episode of a great European myth reveals to us at least one neglected aspect of the symbolism of the Centre: that there is not only an intimate interconnection between the universal life and the salvation of man; but that *it is enough only to raise the question of salvation*, to pose the central problem; that is, *the* problem—for the life of the cosmos to be for ever renewed. For—as this mythological fragment seems to show—death is often only the result of our indifference to immortality.

II

Indian Symbolisms of Time and Eternity

THE FUNCTION OF THE MYTHS

Indian myths are "myths" before they are "Indian"; that is to say, they form part of a particular category of archaic man's spiritual creations and may, therefore, be compared with any other group of traditional myths. So, before dealing with the Indian mythology of Time, it is advisable briefly to recall the intimate connections between the Myth as such, as an original form of culture, and Time. For besides the specific functions that it fulfils in archaic societies, which we need not dwell upon here, the myth is also important in what it reveals to us about the structure of Time. As is generally admitted today, a myth is an account of events which took place *in principio*, that is, "in the beginning", in a primordial and non-temporal instant, a moment of *sacred time*. This mythic or sacred time is qualitatively different from profane time, from the continuous and irreversible time of our everyday, de-sacralised existence. In narrating a myth, one re-actualises, in some sort, the sacred time in which the events narrated took place. (This, moreover, is why the myths, in traditional societies, are not to be narrated however or whenever one likes; they can be recited only during the sacred seasons, in the bush and at night, or around the fire after or before the rituals, etc.) In a word, the myth is supposed to happen—if one may say so—in a non-temporal time, in an instant without duration, as certain mystics and philosophers conceived of eternity.

This observation is important, for it follows that the narration of the myths is not without consequences for him who recites and those who listen. From the mere fact of the narration of a myth, profane time is—at least symbolically—abolished: the narrator and his hearers are rapt into sacred and mythical time. We have tried to show elsewhere[1] that the abolition of profane time by the imitation of exemplary models and the re-enactment of mythical events constitutes, as it were, a specific mark of all traditional societies; and that this mark is, of itself, enough to differentiate the archaic world from that of our modern societies. In the traditional societies men endeavoured, consciously and voluntarily, to abolish Time—periodically to efface the past and to regenerate Time—by a series of rituals which, as it were, re-enacted the cosmogony. We need not enter here into developments which would take us too far from our subject. Enough to remind ourselves that the myth takes man out of his own time—his individual, chronological, "historic" time—and projects him, symbolically at least, into the Great Time, into a paradoxical instant which cannot be measured because it does not consist of duration. This is as much as to say that the myth implies a break-away from Time and the surrounding world; it opens up a way into the sacred Great Time.

Merely by listening to a myth, man forgets his profane condition, his "historical situation" as we are accustomed to call it today. It is not absolutely necessary that a man should belong to a historic civilisation before we can say that he is in a "historical situation". The Australian living upon insects and roots is also living in a "historical situation" in the sense that it is a well-delimited one, expressed in a certain ideology and sustained by a certain type of social and economic organisation: specifically, the existence of the Australian very likely represents a variant of the historical situation of paleolithic man. For the expression "a historical situation" need not necessarily imply "history" in the major sense of the word; it implies only the human condition as such; that is, a condition ruled by a certain system of customs.

[1] See the *Myth of the Eternal Return*, pp. 51 ff. and *passim*.

But not only an Australian, an individual belonging to a much more highly evolved civilisation—a Chinese, for instance, or a Hindu, or a peasant of some European country—when he is listening to a myth, forgets, as it were, his particular situation and is projected into another world, into a Universe which is no longer his poor little universe of every day.

It should be remembered that for each of these individuals, for the Australian as well as for the Chinese, the Hindu and the European peasant, the myths are *true* because they are *sacred*, because they tell him about sacred beings and events. Consequently, in reciting or listening to a myth, one resumes contact with the sacred and with reality, and in so doing one transcends the profane condition, the "historical situation". In other words, one goes beyond the temporal condition and the dull self-sufficiency which is the lot of every human being simply because every human being is "ignorant"—in the sense that he is identifying himself, and Reality, with his own particular situation. And ignorance is, first of all, this false identification of Reality with what each one of us *appears to be or to possess*. A politician thinks that the only true reality is political power, a millionaire is convinced that wealth alone is real, a man of learning thinks the same about his studies, his books, laboratories and so forth. The same tendency is equally in evidence among the less civilised, in primitive peoples and savages, but with this difference, that the myths are still alive amongst them, which prevents them from identifying themselves wholly and completely with non-reality. The periodic recitation of the myths breaks through the barriers built up by profane existence. The myth continually reactualises the Great Time, and in so doing raises the listener to a superhuman and supra-historical plane; which, among other things, enables him to approach a Reality that is inaccessible at the level of profane, individual existence.

INDIAN MYTHS OF TIME

Certain Indian myths furnish particularly happy illustrations of this function of "breaking-through" individual and historical time and realising the mythical Great Time. We will give one famous example, from the *Brahmavaivarta Purāna,* of which the late Heinrich Zimmer gave a summary and commentary in his book, *Myths and Symbols in Indian Art and Civilization.*[2] This text has the merit of beginning straight away with the Great Time as an instrument of knowledge, and thence of deliverance from the bonds of Māyā.

After his victory over the dragon Vritra, Indra decides to rebuild and embellish the residence of the gods. Visvakarman, the divine artificer, succeeds after a year's labour in constructing a magnificent palace. But Indra seems not to be satisfied; he wants the building to be enlarged and to be made still more majestic, unparalleled in all the world. Visvakarman, exhausted by his effort, complains to Brahmā the Creator god, who promises to help him and intercedes with Vishnu the Supreme Being, of whom Brahmā himself is but an instrument. Vishnu undertakes to bring Indra back to his senses.

One fine day, Indra in his palace receives a visit from a boy dressed in rags. This is Vishnu himself, who has assumed this disguise to humiliate the King of the Gods. Without at first revealing his identity to the latter, he calls him "my child" and begins to tell him about the innumerable Indras who, up to that very moment, have peopled the innumerable universes.

" The life and kingship of an Indra endure seventy-one eons [a cycle, a *mahāyuga,* consists of 12,000 divine years or 4,320,000 years!], and when twenty-eight Indras have expired, one day and night of Brahmā have elapsed. But the existence of one

[2] Heinrich Zimmer, *Myths and Symbols in Indian Art and Civilization,* edited by Joseph Campbell, New York, 1946, the Bollingen Series, VI, pp. 3 ff

Brahmā, measured in such Brahmā days and nights, is only one hundred and eight years. Brahmā follows Brahmā; one sinks, the next arises; the endless series cannot be told. There is no end to the number of those Brahmās—to say nothing of Indras.

"But the universes side by side at any given moment, each harbouring a Brahmā and an Indra: who will estimate the number of these? Beyond the farthest vision, crowding outer space, the universes come and go, an innumerable host. Like delicate boats they float on the fathomless, pure waters that form the body of Vishnu. Out of every hair-pore of that body a universe bubbles and breaks. Will you presume to count them? Will you number the gods in all those worlds—the worlds present and the worlds past?"

While the boy was speaking, a procession of ants had appeared in the great hall of the palace. Deployed in a column four yards wide, this mass of ants was parading across the floor. Noticing them, the boy stops, and then, struck with astonishment, suddenly bursts into laughter. "What are you laughing at?" inquires Indra. And the boy replies:

"I saw the ants, O Indra, filing in long parade. Each was once an Indra. Like you, each by virtue of pious deeds once ascended to the rank of a king of gods. But now, through many rebirths, each has become again an ant. This army is an army of former Indras . . ."

This revelation brings home to Indra all the vanity of his pride and ambition. Sending for the wonderful architect Visvakarman, he rewards him royally, and gives up for ever his wish to aggrandise the palace of the gods.

The intention of this myth is transparent. The bewildering evocation of innumerable universes arising from the body of Vishnu and disappearing again is enough of itself to awaken Indra —that is, to make him transcend the limited and strictly conditioned horizon of his "situation" as King of the Gods. One might even be tempted to add "his historical situation", for Indra happened to be the great warrior Chief of the Gods at a certain historic moment, in a definite phase of the great cosmic drama. What Indra hears from the mouth of Vishnu is *a true story*; the true story of the eternal creation and destruction of worlds, beside which his own history, that of his countless heroic adventures culminating in the victory over Vritra, seems, indeed, to be "false"—its events are without transcendent significance. The *true story* reveals to him the Great Time, mythic time in which is the true source of all beings and of all cosmic events. It is because he can thus transcend his historically conditioned "situation", and succeeds in piercing the veil of illusion created by profane time— that is, by his *own* history—that Indra is cured of his pride and ignorance: in Christian terms he is "saved". And this redemptive function of the myth applies not only to Indra, but also to every human being who listens to his adventure. To transcend profane time and re-enter into mythical Great Time is equivalent to a revelation of ultimate reality—reality that is strictly metaphysical, and can be approached in no other way than through myths and symbols.

This myth has a sequel, to which we shall return. For the moment, let us note that the conception of cyclic and infinite Time, presented in so striking a manner by Vishnu, is the general Indian conception of cosmic cycles. Belief in the periodic creation and destruction of the Universe is found as early as in the *Atharva Veda* (X, 8, 39-40). And as a matter of fact it belongs to the *Weltanschauung* of all archaic societies.

THE DOCTRINE OF THE YUGAS

India, however, has elaborated a doctrine of cosmic cycles by amplifying the number of periodic creations and destructions of the Universe to ever more terrifying proportions. The unit of measurement for the smallest cycle of all is the *yuga*—the "age". A *yuga* is preceded by a "dawn" and followed by a "dusk", which fill the intervals between the successive "ages". A complete cycle or *mahāyuga* is composed of four "ages" of unequal duration, the longest appearing at the beginning of a cycle and the shortest at the end of it. The names of these *yuga* are borrowed from the names of the "throws" in the game of dice. *Krita yuga* (from the verb *kri*, to "make" or to "accomplish") means the "perfect age"; in dice-play, the throw that turns up the side with four pips is the winning throw. For in the Indian tradition, the number four symbolises totality, plenitude or perfection. The *krita yuga* is the perfect age, and therefore it is also called the *satya yuga*; that is, the "real", true, or authentic age. From every point of view it is the golden age, the beatific epoch ruled by justice, happiness and prosperity. During the *krita yuga* the moral order of the Universe, the *dharma*, is observed in its entirety. What is more, it is observed spontaneously, without constraint, by all beings, for during the *krita yuga* the *dharma* is in some sort identified with human existence. The perfect man of the *krita yuga* incarnates the cosmic norm, and therefore the moral law. He leads an exemplary, archetypal existence. In other, non-Indian traditions, this golden age is equivalent to the primordial, paradisiac epoch.

The succeeding age, the *tretā yuga* or triad, so named after the die with three pips, marks the beginning of a regression. Human beings no longer observe more than three-quarters of the *dharma*. Work, suffering and death are now the lot of mankind. Duty is no longer performed spontaneously, but has to be learnt. The customs proper to the four castes begin to be altered.

With the *dvāpara yuga* (the age symbolised by "two"), only half of the *dharma* survives on earth. Vices and evils increase, human life becomes of still shorter duration. And in *kali yuga*, the "evil age", only a quarter of the *dharma* remains. The term *kali* designates the die marked with one pip only, which is also the "losing throw" (personified, moreover, as an evil spirit): *kali* signifies also "dispute, discord" and, in general, the most evil of any group of beings or objects. In *kali yuga* man and society reach the extreme point of disintegration. According to the *Vishnu*

Purāna (IV, 24) the syndrome of *kali yuga* is marked by the fact that it is the only age in which property alone confers social rank; wealth becomes the only motive of the virtues, passion and lust the only bonds between the married, falsehood and deception the first condition of success in life, sexuality the sole means of enjoyment, while external, merely ritualistic religion is confused with spirituality. For several thousand years, be it understood, we have been living in *kali yuga*.

The figures 4, 3, 2 and 1 denote both the decreasing length of each *yuga* and the progressive diminution of the *dharma* subsisting in it; to which, moreover, corresponds a shortening of the length of human life, accompanied as we saw by a progressive relaxation of morals and a continuous decline of intelligence. Certain Hindu schools like the *Pāncharātra* connect the theory of cycles with a doctrine about the "decline of knowledge" (*jnāna bhramsa*).

The relative duration of each of these four *yugas* may be calculated in different ways, depending upon the values ascribed to the years—whether they are regarded as human years, or as divine "years", each comprising 360 years. To take a few examples: according to certain sources (*Manu* I, 69 *et seq.*, *Mahābhārata* III, 12, 826), the *krita yuga* lasts for 4,000 years, plus 400 years of "dawn" and as many of "dusk"; then come the *tretā yuga* of 3,000 years, the *dvāpara* of 2,000 years and *kali yuga* of 1,000—all, of course, with their corresponding periods of "dawn" and "dusk". A complete cycle, a *mahāyuga*, therefore comprises 12,000 years. The passage from one *yuga* to another takes place during a twilight interval, which marks a decline even within each *yuga*, every one of them terminating in a phase of darkness. As we are approaching the end of the cycle—that is, the fourth and last *yuga*, the darkness deepens. The final *yuga*, that in which we find ourselves now, is also regarded, more than any other, as the "age of darkness"; for, by a play upon words, it has become associated with the goddess Kālī—the "black". Kālī is one of the multiple names of the Great Goddess, of Shakti the spouse of the god Shiva; and this name of the Great Goddess has naturally been connected with the Sanskrit word *kāla*, "time": Kālī thus becomes not only "the Black", but also the personification of Time.[3] But, etymology apart, the association between *kāla*, "time", the goddess Kālī and *kali yuga* is structurally justifiable: Time is "black" because it is irrational, hard and pitiless; and Kālī, like all the other Great Goddesses, is the mistress of Time, of all the destinies that she forges and fulfils.

A complete cycle, a *mahāyuga*, ends in a "dissolution" or *pralaya*, and this is repeated in a still more radical way at the *mahāpralaya*, or "Great Dissolution", at the end of the thousandth cycle. For later speculation has amplified and multiplied this primordial rhythm of "creation-destruction-creation" *ad infinitum* by projecting the unit of measure—the *yuga*—into vaster and vaster cycles. The 12,000 years of one *mahāyuga* have been counted as "divine years" of 360 years each, which gives a total of 4,320,000 years for a single cosmic cycle. A thousand of such *mahāyugas* constitute one *kalpa* (or "form"); 14 *kalpas* make up one *manvantāra* (so called because each such period is supposed to be governed by a Manu, or mythical ancestor-king). One *kalpa* is equal to one day in the life of Brahmā, and another *kalpa* to one night. A hundred of these "years" of Brahmā, say 311 thousand billion human years, make up the life of the god. But even this considerable length of Brahmā's life does not exhaust the whole of Time, for the gods are not eternal, and the cosmic creations and destructions go on without end.

All we need retain from this cataract of numbers, is the cyclic character of cosmic Time. In fact, what we have here is the repetition to infinity of the same phenomenon (creation-destruction-new creation) prefigured in each *yuga* ("dawn" and "dusk") but completely realised in a *mahāyuga*. The life of Brahmā thus comprises 2,560,000 of these *mahāyugas*, each going through the same stages (*krita, tretā, dvāpara, kali*) and concluding with a *pralaya*, with a *ragnarök* (the "definitive" destruction, or total dissolution

[3] Cf. J. Przyluski, "From the Great Goddess to Kāla", in the *Indian Historical Quarterly*, 1938, pp. 267 ff.

of the cosmic Egg takes place in the *mahāpralaya* at the end of each
kalpa). The *mahāpralaya* implies the regression of all forms and
all modes of existence into the original, undifferentiated *prakriti*.
On the mythical plane nothing remains but the primordial Ocean,
on the surface of which the great god Vishnu sleeps.

Besides the metaphysical depreciation *of human life as history*[4]
—which, by and in proportion to its duration, causes an *erosion*
of all forms, an exhaustion of their ontological substance—and
besides the myth of the *perfection of the beginnings*, a universal
tradition which recurs here too (paradise is lost gradually in this
case, simply because it is *realised*, because it takes *form* and *duration*)
—besides these, what most merits our attention in this orgy of
figures is the *eternal repetition* of the fundamental rhythm of the
Cosmos: its periodical destruction and re-creation. From this
cycle without beginning or end, which is the cosmic manifestation
of *māyā*, man can extricate himself only by an act of spiritual
freedom (for all Indian soteriological systems are reducible to a
previous deliverance from the cosmic illusion, and to spiritual
freedom).

The two great heterodoxies, Buddhism and Jainism, accept the
same Indian doctrine of cyclic time, in its general outlines, and
liken it to a wheel of twelve spokes (an image that occurs earlier
in the Vedic texts, in the *Atharva Veda*, X, 8, 4 and *Rig Veda*, I,
164, 115, etc.). Buddhism adopted the *kalpa* (in Pali, *kappa*) as the
unit of measurement for the cosmic cycles, dividing it into a var-
iable number of what the texts call "incalculables" (*asam-kheya*, in
Pali *asankheyya*). The Pali sources generally mention 4 *asankheyyas*
and 100,000 *kappa* (for example *Jātaka* I, p. 2). In the Mahāyāna
literature the number of "incalculables" varies between 3, 7 and
33, and they are related to the career of the Bodhisattva in the
different Cosmoses. The progressive decadence of man is marked,
in the Buddhist tradition, by a constant diminution of the length of
human life. Thus, according to the *Dīghanikāya* II, 2-7, during the
epoch of the first Buddha, Vipassi, who lived 91 *kappa* ago, the

[4] Further upon all this, see *The Myth of the Eternal Return*, pp. 112 ff. and *passim*.

length of human life was 80,000 years; during that of the second Buddha, Sikhi, 31 *kappa* ago, it was 70,000, and so on. The seventh Buddha, Gautama, made his appearance when human life was no longer than 100 years; that is, when it had been reduced to its absolute minimum. (We find the same idea in the Iranian apocalypses.) However, in Buddhism and in Indian speculation as a whole, time is unlimited; the Bodhisattvas will reincarnate, in order to proclaim the good news of salvation to all beings, for all eternity. The sole possibility of escape from time, of breaking out of the iron ring of existences, is to abolish the human condition and attain Nirvāna. Moreover, all the "incalculables" and all the countless æons also have a soteriological function: the mere contemplation of such a panorama terrifies man, compelling him to realise that he will have to recommence this same transitory existence billions of times over, and endure the same sufferings without end; the effect of which is to stir up his will to escape— that is, to impel him to transcend his condition as an "existant" once and for all.

COSMIC TIME AND HISTORY

Let us consider for a moment this vision of infinite Time, of the endless cycles of creations and destructions, this myth of the eternal return, as an "instrument of knowledge" and a means to liberation. In the perspective of the Great Time every existence is precarious, evanescent and illusory. Seen in the light of the major cosmic rhythms—namely, the *mahāyuga*, the *kalpa* and the *manvantāra*— not only is human existence, and history itself with all its countless empires, dynasties, revolutions and counter-revolutions, manifestly ephemeral and in a sense unreal; the Universe itself vanishes into unreality; for, as we saw, universes are continually being born from the innumerable pores of the body of Vishnu, and disappearing like the bubbles of air that arise and break on the surface of the waters. Existence *in* Time is ontologically a non-existence, an unreality. That is how one has to understand the affirmation of Indian idealism, and of the Vedānta first and fore-most, that this world is illusory, wanting in reality. It lacks reality because of its limited duration; in the perspective of the eternal return it is non-duration. This table here is unreal, not because it does not exist in the strict sense of the term, not because it is an illusion, for it is no illusion that at this precise moment it does exist. But it is illusory in that it will no longer exist ten thousand years hence. The historic world, the societies and civilisations painfully built up by the efforts of countless generations, are all unreal because, in comparison with the cosmic rhythms, they last only for an instant. The Vedantin, the Buddhist, the rishi, the yogi, the sadhu, etc., draw the logical conclusions from the lessons of infinite Time and from the Eternal Return; they renounce the world and seek the absolute Reality; for it is only knowledge of the Absolute that can help them to free themselves from illusion, to pierce the veil of Māyā.

But renunciation of the world is not the only consequence that an Indian is entitled to draw from the discovery of infinite, cyclic Time. As we are now beginning to understand better, India has not known *only* negation and total world-refusal. Starting from this same dogma of the fundamental unreality of the Cosmos, Indian thought also mapped out a way that does not necessarily lead to asceticism and abandonment of the world. Such is the way preached, for instance, by Krishna in the *Bhagavad-Gītā*;[5] the *phalatrisnavairāgya*, which means the "renunciation of the fruits of action"—that is, of the advantages one might gain by one's action, without renouncing the action itself. This is the way illustrated by the sequel to the myth of Vishnu and Indra, whose adventure we have recounted above.

Humiliated by Vishnu's revelation, Indra renounces his voca-tion of warrior-god, and withdraws into the mountains to practise the most terrible asceticism. In other words, he prepares to draw what seems to him the only logical conclusion from the discovery

[5] Cf. for example, *Bhagavad-Gītā* IV, 20; see also our *Yoga, Immortality and Freedom*, New York, 1958, pp. 158 ff.

of the unreality and vanity of the world. He finds himself in the same situation as Prince Siddhārtha immediately after having abandoned his palace and his wives at Kapilavastu and having entered upon his rigorous mortifications. But it is a question whether a King of the Gods and a husband has the right to draw such conclusions from a metaphysical revelation; whether his renunciation and asceticism might not endanger the equilibrium of the world. And indeed, shortly afterwards, his consort the queen Saci, in despair at having been abandoned, implores the help of their spiritual guide Brihaspati. Taking her by the hand, Brihaspati approaches Indra, and speaks to him at length, not only about the virtues of the contemplative life, but also of the life of action, the life that finds its fulfilment in this world of ours. Indra thus receives a second revelation: he now understands that everyone ought to take his own path to the fulfilment of his vocation, which means, in the last reckoning, doing his duty. And, since Indra's vocation and his duty were to continue to be Indra, he resumes his identity and carries on his heroic adventures, but without pride or delusion now that he understands the vanity of all "situations", even that of a King of Gods . . .

This sequel to the myth restores the balance. What is essential is not always to forsake one's historical situation and strive in vain to rejoin the universal Being—it is to keep steadily in mind the perspectives of Great Time, while continuing to fulfil one's duty in historical time. This is precisely the lesson given by Krishna to Arjuna, in the *Bhagavad-Gītā*. In India, as elsewhere in the archaic world, the access to Great Time obtained by the periodic recitation of the myths, permits the indefinite continuance of a certain *order*, which is at once metaphysical, social and ethical. This order does not encourage an idolisation of History, for the perspective of mythical time renders any portion of historic time illusory.

As we have just seen, the myth of cyclic and endless Time, destroying as it does the illusions woven by the minor rhythms of time (that is, by historical time) reveals to us the precariousness and the ontological unreality of the Universe, and, at the same time, it points to the way of deliverance. Indeed, one can be saved from the bonds of Māyā either by the contemplative way, renouncing the world, practising asceticism and the mystical techniques conducive thereto, or by the way of action, remaining in the world, but no longer enjoying the "fruits of one's actions" (*phalatrisnavairāgya*). In either case, the essential thing is not to believe in the reality *exclusively* of the forms that are born and bloom in Time: we must never forget that such forms are "true" only in their own frame of reference and that, ontologically, they are devoid of substance. As we have said, Time can become an instrument of knowledge, in the sense that it is enough to project a thing or a being upon the plane of cosmic Time to become immediately aware of its unreality. The gnoseological and soteriological function of such a change of perspective, obtained by reference to the major rhythms of time, is admirably illustrated by certain myths about the Māyā of Vishnu.

Here is one of these myths, in the popular modern version narrated by Sri Ramakrishna.[6] A famous ascetic named Nārada, having obtained grace of Vishnu by his numberless austerities, the god appears to him and promises to do for him anything he may wish. "Show me the magical power of thy *māyā*," Nārada requests of him. Vishnu consents, and gives the sign to follow him. Presently, they find themselves upon a desert road in hot sunshine, and Vishnu, feeling thirsty, asks Nārada to go on a few hundred yards farther, where there is a little village, and fetch him some water. Nārada hastens forward and knocks at the door of the first house he comes to. A very beautiful girl opens the door; the ascetic gazes upon her at length and forgets why he has come. He enters the house, and the parents of the girl receive him with the respect due to a saint. Time passes, Nārada marries the girl, and learns to know the joys of marriage and the hardships of a peasant

[6] *The Sayings of Sri Ramakrishna*, Madras edition, 1938, Book IV, Chap. 22. See another version of this myth according to the *Matsya Purāna*, recounted by H. Zimmer, *Myths and Symbols*, pp. 27 ff.

life. Twelve years go by: Nārada now has three children, and, after his father-in-law's death, becomes the owner of the farm. But in the course of the twelfth year, torrential rains inundate the region. In one night the cattle are drowned and the house collapses. Supporting his wife with one hand, holding two of his children with the other and carrying the smallest on his shoulder, Nārada struggles through the waters. But the burden is too great for him: he slips, the little one falls into the water; Nārada lets go of the other two children to recover him, but too late; the torrent has carried him far away. Whilst he is looking for the little one, the waters engulf the two others and, shortly afterwards, his wife. Nārada himself falls, and the flood bears him away unconscious, like a log of wood. When, stranded upon a rock, he comes to himself and remembers his misfortunes, he bursts into tears. But suddenly he hears a familiar voice: "My child! Where is the water you were going to bring me? I have been waiting for you more than half an hour!" Nārada turns his head and looks: instead of the all-destroying flood, he sees the desert landscape, dazzling in the sunlight. And the god asks him: "Now do you understand the secret of my *māyā*?"

Obviously Nārada cannot claim to understand it entirely; but he has learned one essential thing: he knows now that Vishnu's cosmic *māyā* is manifested through time.

THE "TERROR OF TIME"

The myth of cyclic Time, of the cosmic cycles repeating themselves *ad infinitum*, is not an invention of Indian speculation. As we have seen elsewhere,[7] the traditional societies—whose representations of Time are so difficult to grasp just because they are conveyed in symbols and rituals whose deeper meaning sometimes remains inaccessible to us—these traditional societies conceive man's temporal existence not only as an infinite repetition of certain archetypes and exemplary gestures, but also as an

[7] *The Myth of the Eternal Return, passim.*

eternal recommencement. Indeed, symbolically and ritually, the world is periodically re-created: the cosmogony is repeated at least once a year—and the cosmogonic myth serves also as the model for a great many actions—marriage, for instance and healing.

What is the meaning of all these myths and all these rites? That the world is born, disintegrates, perishes and is reborn in a very rapid rhythm. Chaos and the cosmogonic act that puts an end to chaos by a new creation are periodically re-enacted. The year—or what we understand by that term—is equivalent to the creation, duration and destruction of a world, of a Cosmos. It is quite probable that this conception of the periodic creation and destruction of the world, although it may have been confirmed by the spectacle of the periodical death and resurrection of vegetation is, for all that, *not* a creation of the agricultural societies. It is also found in the mythologies of pre-agricultural societies, and is very likely a lunar conception. The moon, indeed, measures the most conspicuous periodicities, and it was terms relating to the moon that were first used for the measurement of time. The lunar rhythm regularly presents a "creation" (the new moon), followed by a growth (to full moon), a diminution and a "death" (the three moonless nights). It was very probably the image of the eternal birth and death of the moon which helped to crystallise the earliest human intuitions about the alternations of Life and Death, and suggested, later on, the myth of the periodic creation and destruction of the world. The most ancient myths of the deluge disclose a lunar structure and origin. After every deluge a mythic Ancestor gives birth to a new humanity; and it generally happens that this mythical Ancestor takes on the aspect of a lunar animal. (In ethnology, those animals are called lunar whose life shows a certain alternation; notably that of periodical appearances and disappearances.)

For the "primitive", therefore, Time is cyclic; the world is successively created and destroyed, and the lunar symbolism of "birth-death-resurrection" is present in a great many myths and rites. It was out of such an immemorial heritage that the pan-Indian doctrine of the ages of the world and of the cosmic cycles was elaborated. Of course the archetypal image of the eternally repeated birth, death and resurrection of the moon was appreciably modified by Indian thought. As for the astronomical aspect of the *yuga*, it is probable that this was influenced by the cosmological and astrological speculations of the Babylonians. But these contingent historical influences of Mesopotamia upon India must not now detain us. The important point for us to note is that the Indians, in magnifying ever more audaciously the duration and the numbers of the cosmic cycles, had a soteriological aim in view. Appalled by the endless number of births and rebirths of Universes accompanied by an equally vast number of human births and rebirths ruled by the law of *karma*, the Indian was in a sense *obliged* to seek a way out of this cosmic rotation and these infinite transmigrations. The mystical doctrines and techniques that are directed towards the deliverance of man from sorrow and from the frightful successions of "life, death and rebirth", take over the mythic images of cosmic cycles, amplify and utilise them for their proselytising purpose. By the Indians of the post-Vedic epoch—that is, by the Indians who had discovered the "suffering of existence"—the "eternal return" was equated with the infinite cycle of transmigration ruled by *karma*. This present illusory and transitory world, the world of *samsāra*, of sorrow and ignorance, is the world that unfolds itself under the sign of Time. Deliverance from this world, and the attainment of salvation, are equivalent to deliverance from cosmic Time.

INDIAN SYMBOLISM OF THE ABOLITION OF TIME

Kāla, the Sanskrit word for Time, is used in the sense of periods of ttme and of endless durations as well as that of a certain moment, just as it is in European languages (for instance, " What *time* is it *now* ?"). The earliest texts of all emphasise the temporal character of all the Universes and of all possible existences: "Time has en-

gendered all that has been and all that will be" (*Atharva Veda*,
XIX, 54, 3). In the *Upanishads*, Brahman, the Universal Spirit, the
absolute Being, is conceived both as transcending Time and as the
source and foundation of all that manifests itself in Time: "Lord
of what has been and what will be, he is both today and tomorrow" (*Kena Upanishad*, IV, 13). And Krishna, showing himself to Arjuna as God of the Cosmos, declares: "I am Time, which
in its course destroys the world" (*Bhagavad-Gītā*, XI, 32).

As we know, the *Upanishads* distinguish two aspects of Brahman the Universal Being, "the corporeal and the incorporeal, the
mortal and the immortal, the fixed (*sthita*) and the mobile, etc.,"
(*Brihadāranyaka Upanishad*, II, 3, 1). This amounts to saying that
both the manifest and the non-manifest Universe, as well as the
Spirit in its conditioned and non-conditioned modalities, reside
in the One, in Brahman who contains all polarities and all
opposites. But the *Maitri Upanishad* (VII, 11, 8), when defining
the bi-polarity of the universal Being in the domain of Time,
distinguishes the "two forms" (*dve rupe*) of Brahman—that is, the
aspects of the "two natures" (*dvaitibhāva*) of a single essence (*tad
ekam*)—as "Time and Timelessness" (*kālas-cākalas-ca*). In other
words, Time and Eternity are two aspects of the same Principle:
in Brahman, the *nunc fluens* and the *nunc stans* coincide. The
Maitri Upanishad goes on to say: "What precedes the Sun is
timeless (*akāla*) and undivided (*akala*); but what begins with the
Sun is Time that has divisions (*sakala*), and its form is the Year…"

The expression "what precedes the Sun" may be understood,
cosmologically, as a reference to the epoch before the Creation—
for in the intervals between the *mahāyuga*, or the *kalpa*, in the
great Cosmic Nights, there is no duration at all—but it applies
above all in the metaphysical and soteriological spheres: that is,
it points to the paradoxical situation of the man who obtains
illumination, who becomes a *jivan-mukta*, one who is "liberated
in this life", and thereby rises above Time in the sense that he no
longer participates in duration. Indeed, the *Chāndogya Upanishad*
(III, 11) affirms that for the sage, for the enlightened one, the Sun

stands still: "But after elevation into the zenith it (the Sun) will neither rise nor set any more. It will remain alone in the Centre (*ekala eva madhyhe sthātā*). Hence this text: 'There [namely, in the transcendental world of the *brahman*] it has not set, nor did it ever rise . . .' It neither rises nor sets; once for all (*sakrit*) it stands in heaven, for him who knows the doctrine of the *brahman*."

Here, of course, we are given a concrete image of this transcendence: at the zenith—that is, at the summit of the celestial vault, at the "Centre of the World", the place where the rupture of the planes and communication between the three cosmic zones are possible—the Sun (equated with Time) remains motionless for "him who knows"; the *nunc fluens* paradoxically transforms itself into the *nunc stans*. Illumination and understanding achieve the miracle of an escape from Time. This paradoxical instant of enlightenment is compared, in the Vedic and Upanishadic texts, to lightning. Brahman is understood suddenly, like a flash of lightning (*Kena Upanishad*, IV, 4, 5). "In the thunder-flash is the Truth" (*Kausitaki Upanishad*, IV, 2. We know that the same image of lightning for spiritual illumination occurs in Greek metaphysics and in Christian mysticism).

Let us dwell for a moment upon this mythological image of the zenith which is at the same time the Summit of the World and the "Centre" *par excellence*, the infinitesimal point through which passes the Cosmic Axis (*Axis Mundi*). We have shown in the previous chapter how important this symbolism is for archaic thought.[8] A "Centre" represents an ideal point which belongs not to profane geometrical space, but to sacred space; a point in which communication with Heaven or Hell may be realised: in other words, a "Centre" is the paradoxical "place" where the planes intersect, the point at which the sensuous world can be transcended. But by transcending the Universe, the created world, one also transcends time and achieves *stasis*—the eternal nontemporal present.

[8] Cf. above, pp. 41 ff.

That the act of transcending space is one with that of transcending the flux of time is well elucidated by a myth that describes the Nativity of the Buddha. The *Majjhima-Nikāya* (III, p.123) narrates that "as soon as he was born, the Bodhisattva planted his feet flat on the ground and, turning towards the North, took seven steps, sheltered by a white parasol. He contemplated the regions all around and said, with the voice of a bull—: "I am the highest in the world, I am the best in the world, I am the Eldest in the world; this is my last birth: for me, henceforth, there will never be another existence." This mythical incident in the Buddha's nativity is reproduced, with some variations, in the later literature of the Nikāya-Agama, of the Vinaya, and in biographies of the Buddha.[9] The *sapta padāni*, or seven steps, which take the Buddha to the summit of the world also play a part in Buddhist art and iconography. The symbolism of the "seven steps" is fairly transparent.[10] The expression, "I am the highest in the world" (*aggo'ham asmi lokassa*) refers to the Buddha's *transcendence of space*. He has, in effect, reached the "summit of the world" (*lokkagge*), by mounting the seven cosmic storeys that correspond, as we know, to the seven planetary heavens. But by the same token he has also transcended Time, for, in the Indian cosmology, this summit is the point from which the creation began, and accordingly it is the "oldest" part of the world. That is why the Buddha exclaims: "It is I who am the Eldest of the world" (*jettho'ham asmi lokassa*) for, by reaching the top of the cosmos, *Buddha becomes contemporaneous with the commencement of the world.* Having magically abolished time and the creation, he finds himself in the temporal instant which preceded the cosmogony. The law of the irreversibility of cosmic time, so

[9] In a long note to his translation of the *Mahāprajñāpāramitasastra of Nāgārjuna*, M. Etienne Lamotte has assembled and grouped all the most important texts; cf. *Le Traité de la Grande Vertu de Sagesse de Nāgārjuna*, Vol. I, Louvain, 1944, pp. 6 ff.

[10] Cf. Eliade: *Myths, Dreams and Mysteries*, London, 1960, Chapter VI, section on the "Seven Steps of the Buddha".

terrible to those who are dwelling in illusion, is no longer binding upon the Buddha. For him, time is reversible and can even be anticipated, for the Buddha knows not the past only, but also the future. Not only can he abolish time; it is important to note that he can travel through time backwards (*patiloman* Skr. *pratiloman*) "against the fur", and this will hold good equally for the Buddhist monks and yogis who, before attaining their *Nirvāna* or their *samādhi*, effect a "return backwards" which enables them to know their former lives.

THE "BROKEN EGG"

Besides this image of the Buddha transcending space and time, by traversing the seven cosmic planes right to the "Centre" of the world and simultaneously returning to the a-temporal moment which precedes the creation of the world, there is another image beautifully combining the symbolisms of space and time. Paul Mus, in a remarkable article, has drawn attention to the following text from the *Suttavibhanga*:[11]

"When a hen has laid eggs," says the Buddha, "eight, ten or a dozen; when the hen has sat upon them and kept them warm long enough—then, when one of those chicks, the first one to break the shell with the point of its claw or its beak, comes safely out of the egg, what will they call that chick—the eldest, or the youngest?"—"They will call him the eldest, venerable Gautama, for he is the first-born among them."—"So likewise, O brahman, I alone, among all those who live in ignorance and are as though enclosed and imprisoned in an egg, have burst through this shell of ignorance; I alone in this world have attained to the blessed, the universal dignity of the Buddha. Thus, O brahman, I am the eldest, the noblest among beings."

[11] *Suttavibhanga, Pārājika* I, I, 4; cf. H. Oldenberg, *Le Bouddha* (Trans. A. Foucher), pp. 364-365; Paul Mus, "La Notion de temps réversible dans la mythologie bouddhique", an extract from *l'Annuaire de l'École Pratique des Hautes Études*, Section des Sciences religieuses, 1938-1939, Melun, 1939, p. 13.

"Imagery of a deceptive simplicity," comments Paul Mus. "Rightly to understand it, we must remember that the Brahmanic initiation was regarded as a second birth. The most usual name for an initiate was *dvija*, 'the twice-born'. But birds, serpents, etc., are also given this name, inasmuch as they are born from an egg. The laying of the egg was likened to the 'first birth'—that is, to the natural birth of man; and its hatching corresponded to the supernatural birth of initiation. Moreover, the Brahmanic codes do not fail to decree as a principle that the initiated man is socially superior, the elder of the non-initiated, whatever their relationships of physical age or parentage may be" (Mus, *op. cit.* pp. 13-14).

Nor is that all. "How could they have described the supernatural birth of the Buddha, even metaphorically, by likening it to the breaking of an egg which holds in potentiality the 'First-born' (*jyeshta*) of the Universe, without reminding their hearers of the 'cosmic egg' of Brahmanic tradition—from which there came forth, at the dawn of time, the primordial God of creation, variously entitled the Golden Embryo (*Hiranyagarbha*), the Father or Master of the Creators (*Prajāpati*), Agni (God of fire, and the ritual fire) and as the *brahman* (sacrificial principle, 'prayer', divinised texts of hymns, etc.)?" Now, we know that the "cosmic egg" is "formally identified with the year, symbolic expression of Cosmic Time: so that *samsāra*, another image of cyclic time, reduced to its causes, corresponds exactly to the mythical egg." (Mus, *op. cit.*, p. 14, note 1.)

Thus the act of transcending Time is formulated by a symbolism that is both cosmological and spatial. To break the shell of the egg is equivalent, in the parable of the Buddha, to breaking out of the *samsāra*, out of the wheel of existence—that is, to the transcending *both of cosmic Space and cyclic Time*. In this case too, the Buddha makes use of images analogous to those that the Vedas and the Upanishads have accustomed us to. The sun's standing still at the zenith (in the *Chāndogya Upanishad*) is a spatial symbol that expresses the paradoxical act of escaping from the Cosmos, as forcibly as does the Buddhist symbolism of breaking out of the egg. We shall encounter more of such archetypal images, when we come to describe certain aspects of the practice of Tantric yoga.

THE PHILOSOPHY OF TIME IN BUDDHISM

The symbolism of the Seven Steps of the Buddha and of the Cosmic Egg implies the *reversibility of time*, a paradoxical process to which we shall have to return. But first we must present, in its main outlines, the philosophy of time elaborated by Buddhism, especially by the Mahāyāna.[12] For the Buddhist also, time consists of a continuous flux—*samtāna*—and because of this fluidity of time, every "form" that manifests itself in it is not only transient but also ontologically unreal. The philosophers of the Mahāyāna have commented abundantly on what might be called the instantaneity of time; that is, on the fluidity and, in the last analysis, the non-reality of the present instant which is continually transforming itself into the past, into non-being. For the Buddhist philosopher, writes Stcherbatsky, "existence and non-existence are not different appearances of a thing, they are *the thing* itself". As Santaraksita says: "The nature of any thing is its own momentary stasis and destruction".[13] The destruction that Santaraksita speaks of is not empirical destruction like that of a vase breaking when it falls to the ground, but the intrinsic and continuous annihilation of every existing thing involved in Time. It is for this reason that Vasubandhu writes: "Because of immediate destruc-

[12] The elements of this philosophy will be found in the two volumes by Th. Stcherbatsky, *Buddhist Logic*, Leningrad, 1930-32, ("Bibliotheca Buddhica"); and in the rich memoir of Louis de la Vallée-Poussin, "Documents d'Abhidharma: la Controverse du Temps", in *Mélanges chinois et bouddhiques*, V, Brussels, 1937, pp. 1-158. See also S. Schayer, *Contributions to the Problem of Time in Indian Philosophy*, Cracow, 1938; and Ananda K. Coomaraswamy, *Time and Eternity*, Ascona, 1947, pp. 30 ff.

[13] *Tattvasamgraha*, p. 137; Stcherbatsky, *Buddhist Logic*, I, pp. 94 ff.

tion, there is no [real] motion."[14] Movement, and therefore time itself—duration—is a pragmatic postulate, just as the individual Ego is a pragmatic postulate according to Buddhism; but the concept of motion corresponds to no external reality, for it is "something" of our own construction. The fluidity and moment-ariness of the sensible world, its constant annihilation, is the Mahāyānic formula for expressing the unreality of the temporal world. It has sometimes been inferred from this Mahāyānic con-ception of time that the philosophers of the Greater Vehicle thought of time as discontinuous, that "movement consists of a series of discontinuities" (Stcherbatsky). But, as Coomaraswamy justly remarks (*op. cit.*, p. 60), a line is not made up of an infinite series of points but presents itself as a continuum. Vasubandhu himself says that "the arising of instants is uninterrupted" (*nirantara-ksana-utpāda*). Etymologically, the term *samtāna*, which Stcherbatsky translates by "series", means "continuum".

There is nothing new in all this. The logicians and meta-physicians of the Greater Vehicle did no more than press to their ultimate limits the pan-Indian intuitions about the ontological un-reality of all that exists in Time. Fluidity conceals unreality. The only hope and the one way of salvation is the Buddha, who has revealed the Dharma (the absolute reality) and shown the way to Nirvāna. The sermons of the Buddha tirelessly repeat the central theme of his message: everything that is conditioned is unreal; but he never forgets to add that: "This is not I" (*na me so attā*). For he, the Buddha, is one with the Dharma, and therefore he is "simple, non-composite" (*asamkhata*), he is "a-temporal, timeless" (*akāliko*, as we read in the *Anguttara Nikāya* IV, 359-406). The Buddha repeats many times over that he has "transcended the æons" (*kappātito . . . vipumatto*), that he is "not the man of the æons" (*akkapiyo*)—meaning that he is not engaged in the cyclic

[14] *Abhidarmakosa*, IV, 1, quoted by Coomaraswamy, *op. cit.*, p. 58. See trans-lation and commentary of L. de la Vallée-Poussin, *l'Abhidharmakosa de Vasu-bandhu*, 5 vols., Paris, 1923-1931.

flow of time, that he has passed out of cosmic time.[15] For him, says the *Samyutta Nikāya* (I, 141), "there is neither past nor future" (*na tassa paccha na purattham atthi*). To the Buddha, all times have become present time (*Visuddhi Magga*, 411); in other words, he has abolished the irreversibility of time.

The total present, the eternal present of the mystics, is stasis or non-duration. Expressed in spatial symbols, the non-durational eternal present is *immobility*. And, in fact, to denote the un-conditioned state of the Buddha or of the liberated self (*jivan-mukta*), Buddhism—and Yoga too—use expressions relating to immobility or stasis. "He whose thought is stable" (*thita-citto*; *Dīgha Nikāya* II, 157), "he whose spirit is stable" (*thit'atta*, *ibid.* I, 57), "stable", "motionless", etc. Let us not forget that the first and simplest definition of Yoga is that given by Patanjali himself at the beginning of his *Yoga Sutra* (I, 2): "*yogah cittavrittinirodhah*", "Yoga is the suppression of states of consciousness". But sup-pression is only the final end. The yogi begins by "stopping", by "immobilising" his states of consciousness, his psycho-mental flux. (The most usual meaning of *nirodha* is, moreover, that of "re-striction" or "obstruction", as in the acts of "shutting-up", "enclosing", etc.) We will return again to the effects that this stop-page or immobilisation of states of consciousness may have upon the yogis' experience of time.

He "whose thought is stable" and for whom time no longer flows, lives in an eternal present, in the *nunc stans*. The instant, the present moment, the *nunc*, is called *ksana* in Sanskrit and *khana* in Pali.[16] It is by the *ksana*, by the "moment", that time is measured. But this term has also the meaning of "favourable moment", "opportunity", and for the Buddha it is by means of such a "favourable moment" that one can escape from time. The

Buddha advises us "not to lose the moment" for "those who miss
the moment will lament." He congratulates the monks who
"have seized their moment" (*khano vo patiladdho*) and pities those
"for whom the moment is past" (*khanātitā; Samyuta Nikāya*, IV,
126). This means that after the long journey in cosmic time,
passing through innumerable lives, the illumination is instantaneous (*eka-ksana*). "The instantaneous enlightenment" (*eka-
ksanābhisambodhi*) as it is called by the Mahāyānist authors, means
that the comprehension of Reality comes *suddenly*, like a *flash of
lightning*. The same verbal image of lightning is found in the
Upanishadic texts. Any instant whatever, any *ksana* whatever,
may become the "favourable moment", the paradoxical instant
which suspends duration and throws the Buddhist monk into the
nunc stans, into an eternal present. This eternal present is no longer
a part of time, of duration: it is qualitatively different from our
profane "present"—from that precarious present that peeps out
faintly between two non-entities, the past and the future, and will
cease with our death. The "favourable moment" of enlightenment may be compared with the flash that communicates a
revelation, or with the mystical ecstasy which is prolonged,
paradoxically, beyond time.

IMAGES AND PARADOXES

All the images by means of which we try to express the paradoxical act of "escaping from time" are equally expressive of *the
passage from ignorance to enlightenment* (or, in other words, from
"death" to "life", from the conditioned to the unconditioned, etc.).
Broadly speaking, they may be grouped into three classes: first,
the images that point to the abolition of time, and therefore to enlightenment by *breaking through the planes* (the "broken egg-shell",
the lightning, the seven steps of the Buddha, etc.). Secondly, those
that represent an *inconceivable situation* (the Sun standing still in the
zenith, complete cessation of the flow of states of consciousness,
cessation of breathing in the practice of Yoga, etc.), and, thirdly

and lastly, the contradictory image of the "favourable moment", a fragment of time transfigured into an "instant of illumination". The last two images also suggest a break through the planes, for they symbolise the passage from a normal state at the profane level (the motion of the Sun, the flow of consciousness, etc.), to a paradoxical state (immobility of the Sun, etc.), or imply a transubstantiation taking place within the temporal moment itself. (As we know, the passage from profane duration into sacred time that is brought about by a ritual also implies a "cutting across the planes": the liturgical time is a continuation, not of the profane time in which it occurs, but, paradoxically, of the time when the ritual was last performed.)[17]

The structure of these images need not surprise us. All symbolism of transcendence is paradoxical, impossible to conceive at the profane level. The most usual symbol to express the break through the planes and penetration into the "other world"—the transcendent world, whether that of the living or the dead—is the "difficult passage", the razor's edge. "It is hard to pass over the sharpened blade of the razor—that is how the poets express the difficulties of the way" [leading to the supreme knowledge], affirms the *Katha Upanishad* (III, 14). One recalls the text of the Gospel: "Strait is the gate and narrow is the way which leadeth to Life, and few there be that find it" (*Matt*. VII, 14). Nor do the "strait gate", the "razor edge", the narrow and perilous bridge, exhaust the riches of this symbolism. Other images show us a situation apparently without issue. The hero of a tale of initiation has to go "where the night and the day meet together", or find the door in a wall where none can be seen, or go up to Heaven by a passage that half-opens for only an instant, or pass between two millstones in constant motion, between two rocks that may clash together at any moment, or between the jaws of a monster, etc.[18]

[17] Cf. our *Patterns in Comparative Religion*, pp. 388 ff.
[18] Upon these motifs, see A. B. Cook, *Zeus*, III, 2, Cambridge, 1940, Appendix P. "Floating Islands", pp. 975-1016; Ananda K. Coomaraswamy, "Symplegades", in *Studies and Essays in the History of Science and Learning, offered in*

All these images express the necessity of *transcending the "pairs of opposites"*, of abolishing the polarity that besets the human condition, in order to reach the ultimate reality. As Ananda Coomaraswamy said: "Whoever would transfer from this to the Other-world, or return, must do so in the uni-dimensioned and timeless 'interval' that divides related but contrary forces, between which, if one is to pass at all, it must be 'instantly'" (*Symplegades*, p. 486).

Indeed, for Indian thought, the human condition is defined by the existence of opposites, and liberation from the human condition is equivalent to a non-conditioned state in which the opposites coincide. We remember how the *Maitri Upanishad*, referring to the manifest and unmanifested aspects of Being, distinguishes the "two forms" of Brahman as "Time and the Timeless". By the sage, Brahman is seen as the exemplary model: deliverance is "an imitation of Brahman". This is to say that for "him who knows" Time and the Timeless lose their tension as opposites: they are no longer distinct one from the other. To illustrate this paradoxical situation attained by the abolition of the "pairs of opposites", Indian thought, like all archaic thinking, makes use of images whose very structure includes contradiction (images of the type of "finding a door in a wall where none is visible").

The coincidence of the opposites is still better illustrated by the image of the "instant" (*ksana*) that changes into a "favourable moment". Apparently *nothing distinguishes any moment of profane time from the timeless instant attained by enlightenment*. Rightly to understand the structure and function of such an image, one must remember the dialectic of the sacred: any object whatever may paradoxically become a hierophany, a receptacle of the sacred, while still participating in its own cosmic environment (a *sacred* stone, e.g., remains nevertheless a *stone* along with

---

Homage to George Sarton, New York, 1947, pp. 463, 488; Eliade, *Le Chamanisme et les techniques archaïques de l'extase*, Paris, 1951, pp. 419 ff. and *passim*.

other stones).[19] From this point of view, the image of the "favourable moment" illustrates the paradoxical coincidence of the
opposites even more vividly than do the images of contradictory
situations of the type of the Sun standing still, etc.

TECHNIQUES OF THE "ESCAPE FROM TIME"

The instantaneous enlightenment, the paradoxical leap out of
Time, is obtained at the end of a long discipline which comprises
a philosophy as well as a mystical technique. But let us recall a few
of the techniques designed to arrest the flow of time. The com-
monest, the one that is indeed pan-Indian, is *prāṇāyāma*, the
rhythmicisation of breathing. It should be noted that, although its
ultimate aim is the transcendence of the human condition, the
practice of Yoga begins by restoring and improving that condition, bringing it to an amplitude and majesty that seem unattainable to the profane. We are not, at the moment, thinking
of Hatha Yoga, the express purpose of which is to obtain absolute
mastery of the human body and psyche. For all forms of Yoga
include a preliminary transformation of the profane man—weak,
distracted, enslaved by his body and incapable of real mental
effort—into a glorious Man with perfect physical health, absolute
mastery of his body and of his psycho-mental life, capable of self-
concentration, conscious of himself. It is Man thus made perfect
that Yoga seeks finally to surpass, not only the profane, everyday
man.

In cosmological terms (and to penetrate into Indian thought
one must always use this key), it is by starting from *a perfect
Cosmos* that Yoga sets out *to transcend the cosmic condition as such*—
not by starting from chaos. And the physiology and the psycho-
mental life of the profane man are very like a chaos. Yoga practice
begins by organising this chaos—let us say, by "cosmicising" it.
Prāṇāyāma, by rendering the respiration rhythmic, transforms the

[19] Upon the dialectic of the holy, see Eliade, *Patterns in Comparative Religion*,
pp. 7 ff.

yogin, little by little, into a cosmos:[20] breathing is no longer a-rhythmic, thought ceases to be dispersed, the circulation of the psycho-mental forces is no longer anarchic. But, by working thus upon the respiration, the yogin works directly upon the time that he is living. There is no adept in Yoga who, during these exercises, has not experienced quite another quality of time. In vain have they tried to describe this experience of the time lived during *prānāyāma*: it has been compared to the moment of bliss that comes when listening to good music, to the rapture of love, to the serenity or plenitude of prayer. What seems certain is that, by gradually slowing down the respiratory rhythm, prolonging the inhalations and exhalations more and more, and leaving as long an interval as possible between these two movements, the yogin lives in a time that is different from ours.[21]

[20] Cf. my "Cosmic homology and Yoga" in the *Journal of the Indian Society of Oriental Art*, Calcutta, 1937, pp. 188-203. Upon *prānāyāma*, see *Yoga, Immortality and Freedom*, pp. 53 ff.

[21] It may be, indeed, that this rhythmic breathing has a considerable effect upon the yogin's physiology. I have no competence in this domain; but I have been struck, at Rishikesh and elsewhere in the Himalayas, by the admirable physical state of the yogins, who took hardly any nourishment. At my *kutiar* at Rishikesh one of my neighbours was a *naga*, a naked ascetic who spent almost the whole night practising *prānāyāma*, and who never ate more than a handful of rice. He had the body of a perfect athlete; he showed no sign of under-nourishment or fatigue. I wondered how it was that he was never hungry. "I live only by day," he told me; "during the night, I reduce the number of my respirations to a tenth." I am not too sure that I understand what he meant; but may it not simply be that, the vital duration being measured by the number of inhalations and exhalations, which he reduced to a tenth of the normal number during the night, he was living, in 10 hours of our time, only one tenth as long—namely, one hour? Reckoning by the number of respirations, the day of 24 solar hours was lived, by him, in no more than 12 to 13 breathing-hours: by the same measure, *he was eating a handful of rice, not every 24 hours, but every 12 or 13 hours*. This is only a hypothesis which I do not insist upon. But so far as I know, no one has yet given a satisfactory explanation of the astonishing *youthfulness* of some yogins.

Two points seem specially important about this practice of *prāṇāyāma*: first, that the yogin begins by "cosmicising" his body and his psycho-mental life; secondly, that by *prāṇāyāma* the yogin succeeds in putting himself at will into different rhythms of lived time. Patanjali, in his very concise manner, recommends "the control of the moments and of their continuity" (*Yoga Sutra*, III, 52). The later Tantric Yoga treatises give more details about this "control" of time. The *Kālacakra Tantra*, for instance, goes so far as to relate the in-breathing and the out-breathing to the day and the night, and then with the fortnights, the months and the years, and so on, up to the greatest cosmic cycles.[22] This means that the yogin, by his respiratory rhythm, repeats and, in a sense, relives Cosmic Great Time, the periodic creations and destructions of the universes. This exercise has a dual aim: on the one hand, the yogin is brought to identify his own respiratory moments with the rhythms of cosmic time, and in so doing realises the unreality of time. But on the other hand, he obtains the reversibility of the flow of time (*sāra*) in the sense that he returns upon his tracks, he re-lives his previous lives and "burns up" (as the texts put it) the consequences of his previous actions—he annuls these actions, and so escapes from their karmic consequences.

We can discern in such an exercise of *prāṇāyāma*, the will to relive the rhythms of cosmic Great Time; it is, in one sense, the same experience as that of Nārada that we have recounted above, an experience realised, this time, voluntarily and consciously. The proof that this is so, lies in the assimilation of the two "mystical veins", *ida* and *pingala*, to the Moon and the Sun.[23] As we know,

[22] *Kālacakra Tantra*, quoted by Mario E. Carelli in the preface to his edition of the *Sekoddesatākā of Nadapāda (Nāropā)*, *being a commentary of the Sekoddesa Section of the Kālacakra Tantra*, Gaekwad Oriental Series, Vol. XC, Baroda, 1941, pp. 16 ff.

[23] See the texts collected by P. C. Bagchi, "Some technical terms of the Tantras" in *The Calcutta Oriental Journal*, I, 2, November 1934, pp. 75-88, esp. pp. 82 ff.; and Shashibhusan Dasgupta, *Obscure Religious Cults*, Calcutta, 1946, pp. 274 ff.

ida and *pingala* are the two channels in which the psycho-vital energy circulates through the human body. The assimilation of these two mystical veins to the Sun and the Moon perfects the operation that we called the "cosmicising" of the yogin. His mystical body becomes a microcosm; his in-breathing corresponds to the course of the Sun, that is, to the Day; his out-breathing to the Moon, that is, to the Night. Thence it is that the yogin's respiratory rhythm becomes perfectly integrated with the rhythm of cosmic Great Time.

But this integration with cosmic Great Time does not abolish Time as such; it is only the rhythms that are changed. The yogin lives a cosmic Time, nevertheless he continues to live in Time. His ultimate aim, however, is to go out of Time; and that is, in effect, what happens when he succeeds in uniting the two currents of psycho-vital energy circulating through *ida* and *pingala*. By a process too difficult to explain in few words, the yogin stops his respiration and, by unifying the two currents, concentrates them and forces them to circulate through the third "vein"—the *sushumnā*, the vein that is in the "centre". And the *sushumnā*, says the *Hathayoga-pradīpikā* (IV, 16-17), "devours Time". This paradoxical unification of the two mystical veins *ida* and *pingala*, the two polar currents, is equated with the union of the Sun and the Moon—that is, with the abolition of the Cosmos and the re-integration of the opposites; which amounts to saying that the yogin transcends both the created Universe and the Time that governs it. We may recall the mythological image of the egg whose shell is broken by the Buddha. The same thing happens to the yogin who "concentrates" his breathing into the *sushumnā*: he breaks the envelope of his microcosm and transcends the conditioned world which exists in Time. A good many yogic and Tantric texts allude to this non-conditioned and non-temporal state in which there is "neither day nor night" and where "there is no more disease or old age"—naïve and approximate formulas for the "escape from Time". To transcend "the day and the night" means *to transcend the opposites*; it corresponds, on the temporal

plane, to the passage through the "strait gate" on the spatial
plane. In Tantric Yoga this experience prepares and precipitates
the *samādhi*, a state that is usually translated by "ecstasy", but I
would prefer to render it by "enstasis". The yogin ultimately
becomes a *jivan-mukta*, "liberated in this life". We cannot describe his mode of existence, for it is paradoxical. The *jivan-
mukta* is said to live no longer in Time—in our time—but in an
eternal present, in the *nunc stans*, to use the term by which Boeth-
ius defined eternity.

But the Tantric Yoga process that we have just outlined does
not exhaust the Indian techniques of "escape from Time". From a
certain point of view, one might even say that Yoga, as such,
aims at deliverance from the slavery of Time. Every Yoga
technique of concentration or meditation "isolates" the practit-
ioner, withdraws him from the flux of psycho-mental life, and
consequently lessens the pressure of Time. Furthermore, the yogin
is striving to "destroy the sub-consciousness", to "burn up" the
vāsanās. "The *vāsanās* have their origin in the memory", writes
Vyāsa (in his commentary on the *Yoga Sutra*, IV, 9); and this refers
not only to the individual memory, which, for the Hindu, includes both the memories of one's present existence and the
karmic residues of one's innumerable past lives. The *vāsanās*
represent also the entire collective memory transmitted by
language and tradition; they are, in a sense, the "collective unconscious" of Professor Jung.

In striving to modify the subconscious, and ultimately to
"purify", "burn up" and "destroy" it,[24] the yogin is seeking to
free himself from memory", that is, *to abolish the work of Time*. Nor
is this a speciality of Indian disciplines only. A mystic of the
eminence of Meister Eckhardt never ceases to repeat that "there

[24] This may appear a vain, if not a dangerous, presumption in the eyes of
Western psychologists. While disclaiming any right to intervene in the debate,
I would recall, on the one hand, the extraordinary psychological science of the
Hindu yogins, and, on the other hand, the ignorance of Western scientists con-
cerning the psychological reality of the yogins' experiences.

is no greater obstacle to Union with God than Time", that Time hinders man from knowing God, etc. And in this connection it is not without interest to recall that the archaic societies periodically "destroy" the world in order to "remake" it, and thereafter to live in a "new" Universe, without "sin"—meaning without "history", without _memory_. A great many periodic rituals are also directed to collective "purging" from sins (by public confessions, the scape-goat ceremony, etc.), in the last analysis to the _abolition of the past_. All this proves, I think, that there is no break in continuity between the man of the archaic societies and the mysticisms attaching to the great historic religions: both are striving with the same strength, though by different means, against _memory_ and Time.

But this metaphysical depreciation of Time and this struggle against _memory_ do not represent the whole of the attitude of Indian spirituality towards Time and History. Let us remember the teaching of the myths of Indra and of Nārada: Māyā manifests in Time, but Māyā herself is only the creative force, above all the cosmogonic force, of the Absolute Being (Siva or Vishnu), which means that in the final reckoning _the great cosmic Illusion is a hierophany_. This Truth, revealed in the myths by a series of images and narratives, is more systematically expounded in the _Upanishads_[25] and the later philosophies: namely, that the ultimate foundation of things, the _Ground_, is constituted by both Māyā and the Absolute Spirit, by the Illusion and the Reality, by Time and Eternity. By identifying all the "opposites" in the one and only universal Void (_sunya_), certain Mahāyānic philosophers (Nāgārjuna, for example) and above all the various Tantric schools, Buddhist (Vajrayāna) as well as Hindu, have come to similar conclusions. All this is unlikely to surprise anyone who knows how Indian spirituality longs to transcend the opposites and the polar tensions, to unify the Real and reintegrate the primordial One. If Time, seen as Māyā, is itself a manifestation of the Divinity, to live in Time is not in itself a "bad action": "bad action" is _to_

[25] Cf. above, pp. 74 ff.

believe that nothing else exists, nothing outside of Time. One is
devoured by Time, not because one lives in Time, but because one
believes in its *reality,* and therefore forgets or despises eternity.

This is no unimportant conclusion; all too often we tend to
reduce Indian spirituality to its extreme positions, which are
highly "specialised" and for that reason inaccessible except to the
sages and mystics, forgetting the universal Indian teachings
illustrated, above all, by the myths. It is true that the "escape
from Time" attained by the *jivan-mukta* amounts to an "enstasis"
or ecstasy unattainable by the majority of human beings. But
though this "escape from Time" remains the royal road to
deliverance (let us remember the symbols of instantaneous
illumination, etc.), this does not mean that all those who do not
attain to it are irretrievably condemned to ignorance and bondage.
As the myths of Indra and Nārada show us, even to make oneself
conscious of the ontological unreality of Time, and to "realise"
the rhythms of cosmic Great Time, is enough to free oneself from
illusion. So, to sum it up, India recognises not only two possible
situations with regard to Time—that of the ignorant who live
exclusively in duration and illusion, and that of the Sage or the
yogin who are striving to "escape from Time"—but also a third,
intermediate situation—that of the man who, while continuing
to live in his own time (historic time), keeps a way open into the
Great Time, never losing consciousness of the unreality of historic
time. That situation, exemplified by Indra after his second
revelation, is fully elucidated in the *Bhagavad-Gītā.* It is expounded above all in the spiritual literature written by modern
Indian masters for the laity. It is not without interest to observe
that this Indian position is in a certain sense a continuation of
primitive man's attitude towards Time.

III

The " God who Binds "
and the Symbolism of Knots

We know the part that is assigned by M. Dumézil to the Terrible
Sovereign of the Indo-European mythologies. On the one hand,
at the very heart of the function of sovereignty, it is opposed to
that of the Sovereign Law-giver (Varuna is opposed to Mitra,
Jupiter to Fides); and on the other hand, compared with the
warrior-gods who always fight by military means, the Terrible
Sovereign has a kind of monopoly of another weapon—magic.
"So there are no mythical combats about Varuna, who is nevertheless the most invincible of the gods. His supreme weapon is his
'*māyā of Asura*', his magic as Sovereign creator of forms and of
marvels, which also enables him to administer the world and keep
it in balance. This weapon is, moreover, depicted in most cases in
the form of a noose, of a knot, of material or figurative bonds
(*pāsā*). The warrior-god, on the contrary, is Indra, a fighting god,
wielder of the thunderbolt and the hero of innumerable duels, of
perils encountered and victories hard-won." The same opposition
can be observed in Greece: whilst Zeus fights and wages difficult
wars, "Ouranos does not fight; there is no trace of a struggle in
his legend, although he is the most terrible of kings and the least
easily dethroned: in his infallible grasp he immobilises—more
exactly, he 'binds', he chains up—his eventual rivals in hell." In the
Nordic mythologies, "Odin is certainly the governor, the warrior-
chief in this world and the next. Yet neither in the prose *Edda* nor
in the *Edda* poems does he himself fight. . . . He has a whole series

of magical 'gifts'—that of ubiquity, or at least of instantaneous transport; the art of disguise and the gift of unlimited metamorphosis; lastly and chiefly, the gift of being able to blind, deafen or paralyse his adversaries and deprive their weapons of all efficacy."[1] Finally, in the Roman tradition, the magical proceedings of Jupiter, intervening in battle as an all-powerful sorcerer, are opposed to the normal, purely military measures of Mars:[2] and this opposition, in India, sometimes manifests itself still more clearly. Indra, for example, rescues the victims "bound" by Varuna and "unlooses "them.[3]

As one might expect, M. Dumézil looks for verification of this polarity of "binder" and "loosener" in the more concrete forms of rites and customs. Romulus, "a tyrant as terrible as marvellous, who binds with all-powerful bonds, founder of the wild Luperci and the frantic Curiaces",[4] is the equivalent, upon the "historicised" plane of Roman mythology, to Varuna, to Ouranos and Jupiter. All Romulus's history and the socioreligious institutions he is supposed to have founded can be explained in terms of the archetype of which he is, in a sense, the incarnation—the Indo-European Magician-King, master of the spells that "bind". M. Dumézil reminds us of a text of Plutarch's (*Romulus*, 26) where it is said that certain men always walked in front of Romulus, "men armed with rods for keeping back the crowd, and girded with straps, ready to bind at once those whom he ordered them to bind".[5] The Luperci, a magico-religious

[1] Georges Dumézil, *Mythes et Dieux des Germains*, Paris, 1939, pp. 21 ff., 27 ff.; *Jupiter, Mars, Quirinus*, Paris, 1941, pp. 79 ff.; cf. *Ouranós-Varuna*, Paris, *passim*.

[2] Dumézil, *Mitra-Varuna*, Paris, 1940, p. 33; *Jupiter, Mars, Quirinus*, pp. 81 ff.

[3] Dumézil, *Flamen-Brahman*, Paris, 1935, pp. 34 ff.; *Mitra-Varuna* pp. 79 ff.

[4] Dumézil, *Horace et les Curiaces*, 1942, p. 68.

[5] *Mitra-Varuna*, p. 72. Again, according to Plutarch (*Rom.* quest. 67), the name itself, *lictores*, is derived from *ligare*, and M. Dumézil sees no reason to "reject the relation that the ancients felt between *lictor* and *ligare*: lictor may have been formed from a verbal root *ligere*, no longer known, which would have been to *ligare* what *dicere* is to *dicare*" (*ibid.* p. 72).

brotherhood founded by Romulus, belonged to the order of the *equites*, and in that capacity they wore a ring on the finger.[6] On the other hand, the *flamen dialis*, representing the austere, juridical, static religion, was allowed neither to ride a horse (*equo dialem flaminem vehi religio est*)[7] nor to "wear a ring unless it were of open-work and hollow" (*item annulo uti, nisi pervio cassoque, fas non est*). "If a man in chains comes in [to the *flamen dialis*] he must be set free: let the shackles be thrown up through the compluvium on to the roof and thrown thence into the street. He [the *flamen*] wears no knot either on his hat, at the belt or elsewhere (*nodum in apice neque in cinctu neque in alia parte ullum habet*). If a man is being led forth to be beaten with rods, and this man throws himself for mercy at the feet of the *flamen*, it is a sacrilege to beat him on that day."[8]

There is no question here of taking up the dossier collected and admirably analysed by M. Dumézil. Our purpose is quite different: we mean to trace, over a still wider field of comparison, the themes of the "god who binds" and of the magic of "binding", by trying to clarify what they mean, and also to define their functions in religious contexts other than that of Indo-European magical sovereignty. I will not pretend to exhaust this enormous material, upon which several monographs have already appeared.[9] What I intend is something of a rather more methodical nature.

[6] *Mitra-Varuna*, p. 16.

[7] Aulus-Gellius, *Noctes Atticae*, X, 15.

[8] Aulus-Gellius, *ibid.*, X, 15; cf. Servius, in *Aen.*, III, 607; see J. Heckenbach, *De nuditate sacra sacrisque vinculis*, R.V.V., X, 3, Giessen, 1911, pp. 69 ff.; Dumézil, *Flamen-Brahman*, pp. 66 ff.

[9] One should mention, after the somewhat disappointing book of Heckenbach, Frazer's *Taboo and the perils of the soul*, pp. 296 ff.; I. Scheftelowitz, *Das Schlingen- und Netzmotiv im Glauben und Brauch der Völker*, R.V.V., XII, 2, Giessen, 1912; the same author's *Altpersische Religion und das Judentum*, Giessen, 1920, pp. 92 ff.; and the studies in ethnology and folk-lore mentioned by Dumézil, *Ouranós-Varuna*, p. 52, note 1. Upon the Roman *nexum*, magical knots and the penal law, cf. Henri Decugis, *Les Étapes du droit*, 2nd edn., Paris, 1946, vol. I, pp. 157-178.

Making use, on the one hand, of the rich collections of facts
amassed by the ethnologists and the historians of religions, and, on
the other, of the results of M. Dumézil's researches in the special
domain of the Indo-European magic of sovereignty, I shall inquire, first: In what sense is the notion of the sovereign who
"binds" specific to, and characteristic of, the Indo-European
religious system? And secondly: What is the magico-religious
content of all the myths, rites and superstitions centred upon this
motive of "binding"? I am not unaware of the dangers involved
in such a project, more especially of the "confusionism" so
brilliantly denounced by M. Dumézil.[10] But here my concern will
be not so much to explain the Indo-European facts by heteroclite
parallels, as to draw up a summary account of the magico-
religious "complexes" of the same type and to specify, as far as
possible, the relations between the Indo-European symbolism of
"binding" and the systems that are morphologically similar
to it. We shall then be in a position to judge whether such a
comparison may be of interest for the history of religion in
general, and of the Indo-European religions in particular.

THE SYMBOLISM OF VARUNA

Like Bergaigne and Güntert before him, M. Dumézil has noted
the magic power of Varuna. This god is verily a "past-master of
bonds"; and many hymns and ceremonies have no other purpose
but to liberate man from the "toils of Varuna".[11] Sāyana, com-
menting on the text of the *Rig Veda* I, 89, 3, explains the name of
Varuna by the fact that he "envelops, which is to say that he
imprisons, the wicked in his toils". "O deliver from their bonds
those who are bound!" (*Atharva Veda* VI, 121, 4.) The bonds of
Varuna are attributed also to Mitra and Varuna together (*Rig
Veda* VII, 65, 3: "they have many bonds ...," etc.) and even to the
whole group of the Adityas (*Rig Veda* II, 27, 16: "Your bonds

[10] In his *Naissance de Rome*, 1944, pp. 12 ff.
[11] For examples—*Rig Veda* I, 24, 15; VI, 74, 4; VII, 65, 3; X, 85, 24, etc.

prepared for the perfidious, for the deceiver . . ."). But it is
Varuna above all who has the magic power to bind and unbind
men at a distance;[12] so much so, that his name itself has been
explained by this faculty of binding: instead of the traditional
etymology—*varu-vrinoti*, "to cover", "to enclose"—which gave
prominence to his ouranian character, we now prefer to follow
the derivation proposed by Petersson and accepted by Güntert
(*op. cit.*, p. 144) and by Dumézil (*Ouranós-Varuna*, p. 49), which has
recourse to another Indo-European root, *uer*, "to bind" (Sanskrit
varatrā, "strap" or "cord"; Lettish *wéru, wert*, "to thread", to
"embroider"; Russian *verenica*, an "unbroken line").[13] Varuna is
represented with a cord in his hand,[14] and in the ceremonies
everything that ties, beginning with the knots, is called Varun-
ian.[15] M. Dumézil ascribes this magical prestige of the master
binder to Varuna's sovereignty. "The bonds of Varuna are also
magical, as Sovereignty itself is magical; they symbolise those
mystic forces retained by the chieftain, which are called Justice,
administration, the royal and public security and all the 'powers'.
Sceptre and bonds, *danda* and *pasah*, share, in India as elsewhere, in
the privilege of representing all this" (*Ouranós-Varuna*, p. 53).

That is correct, without doubt. But neither the "sovereign"
nor even the "sovereign-magician" accounts for the whole of the
complex nature presented by Varuna from the time of the
earliest Vedic texts. If he cannot be classed exclusively among the
"gods of the sky" he nevertheless has qualities proper to the

[12] A. Bergaigne, *La Religion védique d'après les hymnes du Rig Veda* III, Paris,
1883, pp. 114, 157 ff.; H. Güntert, *Der arische Weltkönig und Heiland*, Halle,
1923, pp. 120 ff.; Dumézil, *Ouranós-Varuna*, p. 50. Same attribute in the
Brāhmanas, see Silvain Lévi, *La doctrine du Sacrifice dans les Brāhmanas*, Paris,
1898, pp. 153 ff.

[13] Cf. Walde-Pokorny, *Vergleichendes Wörterbuch der Indogermanischen Sprachen*
I, 1930, p. 263.

[14] Bergaigne, *op. cit.*, III, p. 114; S. Lévi, *op. cit.*, p. 153; E. W. Hopkins, *Epic
Mythology*, Strasbourg, 1920, pp. 116 ff.

[15] Silvain Lévi, *op. cit.*, p. 153; Dumézil, *Ouranós-Varuna*, p. 51, Note 1.

ouranian divinities. He is *visva-darsata*, "everywhere visible", he "separated the two worlds", the wind is his breath; Mitra and he are worshipped as "the two potent and sublime masters of Heaven", who "in the various-coloured clouds show themselves at the first rumble of thunder and make Heaven rain by a divine miracle".[16] This cosmic structure soon enabled him to acquire such lunar[17] and watery characteristics that he became, in time, a god of the Ocean.[18] The same cosmic and ouranian structure explains other functions and magical powers of Varuna; his omniscience, for instance, and his infallibility. He is *sahasrāksa*, the "thousand-eyed",[19] a mythic formula which refers to the stars and—originally, at least—could have been used of none but an ouranian divinity. The magic powers of sovereignty accrued later and multiplied the celestial attributes: Varuna *sees* and *knows* everything, for he rules the world from his starry dwelling; and at the same time he can *do* anything, since he is the cosmocrat, and he punishes by "bondage" (that is, by illness or impotence) anyone who infringes the law, and is guardian of the universal order. There is thus a remarkable symmetry between what might be called the "celestial stratum" and the "royal stratum" of Varuna, which correspond with and complement one another: Heaven is transcendent and unique, exactly as the Universal Sovereign is; the tendency to be passive, manifested by all the supreme gods of Heaven,[20] goes very well with the "magical" prestige of the sovereign gods who "act without action", who work directly by the "power of the spirit".

The structure of Varuna is complex, but he always has structure—that is to say, there is an intimate coherence of all his different modalities. Whether cosmocratic or ouranian, he is

---

[16] *Rig Veda*, VIII, 41, 3; VII, 86, 1; VII, 87, 2; V, 63, 2-5.

[17] Hillebrand, *Vedische Mythologie*, Breslau, 1902, III, p. 1 ff.

[18] S. Lévi, *op. cit.*, pp. 158 ff.; J. J. Meyer, *Trilogie altindische Mächte und Feste der Vegetation*, Zürich-Leipzig, 1937, pp. 206 ff., 269 ff.

[19] *Atharva Veda* IV, 16, 2-7, etc.; *Rig Veda*, I, 35, 7 ff.; *Rig Veda*, VII, 34, 10.

[20] See my *Patterns in Comparative Religion*, pp. 38 ff.

always all-seeing, all-powerful and, at need, "binding" by his "spiritual power"—by magic. But his cosmic aspect is yet more substantial; he is not only, as we saw, a god of Heaven but also a lunar and aquatic god. In Varuna, perhaps from very early times, there was something predominantly "nocturnal" which Bergaigne and, more recently, Ananda Coomaraswamy[21] did not fail to point out. Bergaigne (*loc. cit.*, p. 213) mentions the remark of the commentator of the *Taittirīya Samhitā* (I, 8, 16, 1) that Varuna designates "him who envelops like the darkness". This "nocturnal" side of Varuna is not to be interpreted solely in the ouranian sense of the nocturnal heavens, but also in a wider, truly cosmological and even metaphysical sense. The Night itself *is* virtuality, seed, the non-manifest; and it is just this "nocturnal" modality of Varuna that enabled him to become a god of the Waters (Bergaigne, III, p. 128) and made possible his assimilation to the "demon" Vritra. This is not the place to enter upon the problem of "Vritra-Varuna", and we will do no more than remind ourselves that these two entities have more than one characteristic in common. Even if we ignore the probable etymological relationship between the two names,[22] it is a point of importance that both are found in references to the Waters, and especially to the "contained Waters" ("the great Varuna has hidden the sea . . ." *R.V.* IX, 73, 3); and that Vritra, like Varuna, is sometimes called *māyin*, "magician".[23] From one point of view,

---

[21] Especially in "The Darker Side of the Dawn", *Smithsonian Miscellaneous Collections*, Vol. 94, No. 1, Washington, 1935; and *Spiritual Authority and Temporal Power in the Indian Theory of Government*, American Oriental Society, New Haven, 1942.

[22] Bergaigne, *op. cit.*, III, p. 115, etc.; Coomaraswamy, *Spiritual Authority* . . . pp. 29 ff.

[23] For example, *R.V.* II, 11, 10; cf. [E. Benveniste—] L. Renou, (*Vritra and Vrithragna*, Paris 1934) who is mistaken in saying that "the magic of Vritra answers to that of Indra and is derived from it". *A priori*, the magic is that of ophidian beings—of whom Vritra is most certainly one—rather than of the hero gods. We will come back later to the magic of Indra.

these various assimilations of Vritra and Varuna, like all the other modalities and functions of Varuna, correspond with and justify one another. The Night (the non-manifest), the Waters (the virtual, the seed), "transcendence" and "non-activity" (all characteristics of the heavenly and sovereign gods) are mythically and at the same time metaphysically related to the "bonds" on the one hand, and on the other to Vritra who has "contained", "arrested" or "imprisoned" the Waters. Upon the cosmic plane Vritra, too, is a "binder". Like all the great myths, that of Vritra is multivalent, and cannot be exhaustively interpreted in one sense alone. We can even say that one of the principal functions of the myth is to unify planes of reality which, to immediate consciousness and even to reflection, seem to be multiple and heterogeneous. Thus, in the myth of Vritra, we find, besides other valencies, that of a return to the non-manifested, an "arrest", a "bondage" which prevents further generation of "forms"—that is, of cosmic Life. It would not, of course, be right to make too much of the connection between Vritra and Varuna. But there is an undeniable structural relationship between the "nocturnal", the "non-active", the magician Varuna who from a distance ensnares the guilty,[24] and the Vritra who "chains up" the Waters. The action of both has the effect of "arresting" life, of bringing on death—upon the individual plane in one case, and the cosmic plane in another.

"BINDING GODS" IN ANCIENT INDIA

Varuna is not the only god of ancient India who "binds". Among those who make use of this magic weapon we find Indra, Yama and Nirrti. For instance, it is said of Indra that he brought a "bond" for Vritra (R.V. II, 30, 2) and bound him without cords

[24] We are even tempted to see this means of chastisement as an extension and deepening of what is most typical of Varuna, in the sense that it forces the culprit to a "regression into the virtual, into immobility"—the state which, in a way, Varuna himself represents.

(II, 13, 9). But Bergaigne, who refers to these texts (*op. cit.*, III, p. 115, note 1), observes that "this is evidently only a secondary development of the myth, the meaning of which is that Indra turns the demon's own tricks against him". It is not only Varuna and Vritra who have their *māyā*, but other divine beings as well.[25] But, on the one hand, here we often have to do with religious beings who are ambivalent (Tvashtri, Maruts) in the sense that a demonic element co-exists in them with the divine elements; and, on the other hand, the attribute "magician" is not specific, but is only attached to the divine personalities as an additional honour. Such is the prestige of the *māyin* that it is felt to be necessary to ascribe it to every divinity one wishes to praise. This is a phenomenon well known in the history of religions, especially of the Indian religions, when the "imperialist" tendency impels a successful religious form to assimilate to itself all sorts of other divine attributes and to extend its sway over different areas of the sacred. In the case we are considering, this tendency to annex prestige and powers outside the god's own sphere is all the more interesting since it is the annexation of an archaic religious structure—namely, the prestige of the "magician." And the god who has profited most by it is Indra. "He has overcome the *māyin* by means of *māyā*"—such is the theme of numerous texts (Bergaigne III, p. 82). Foremost among Indra's "magical" powers is that of transformation; but perhaps there may be grounds for distinguishing the many particular epiphanies (a bull, etc.) from the indefinite magical power that enables any being, divine, demonic or human, to assume any animal form whatever. Between the spheres of mythic-religious epiphany and of metamorphosis there are, of course, interchanges, borrowings and confusions; and in so unstable a domain as Vedic mythology it is not always easy to distinguish what belongs to one or the other. But it is just the imprecision and instability that are instructive

[25] Such as the Maruts (*R. V.* V, 53, 6), Tvashtri (X, 53, 9), Agni (I, 44, 1; etc.), Soma (IX, 73, 5; etc.) and even the Açvins (V, 78, 6; etc.; cf. Bergaigne, III, pp. 80 ff.).

from a phenomenological point of view, showing up as they do
the tendency of religious "forms" to interpenetrate and absorb
one another, and this dialectical process can even help us to understand archaic religious phenomena.

To return to Indra: he is not only in certain cases a "magician",
he also "binds" just as Varuna and Vritra do. The atmosphere is
his snare, in which he envelops his enemies (*A.V.* VIII, 8, 5-8, etc.).
The corresponding Iranian god, Verethragna, binds the hands of
his adversary (*Yasht*, 14, 63). But those are secondary features,
possibly to be explained by the known prehistoric use of the
lasso as a weapon of war. It is true that according to archaic thinking, a weapon is always a *magical means*, but that does not prevent
a god who is definitely a warrior, like Indra, from using this
magical means in actual combat, whereas Varuna uses his "bonds"
without fighting, without acting—but magically.

More instructive is the example of the other binding gods,
Nirrti and Yama, both divinities of death. The bonds of Yama
(*A.V.* VI, 96, 2; VIII, 7, 28) are generally called the "bonds of
death" (*A.V.* VII, 112, 2; VIII, 2, 2, etc.). As for Nirrti, he binds
those he means to destroy (*A.V.* VI, 63, 1-2; *Taitt. Sam.*, V, 2, 4,
3; *Satapatha Brāhmana*, VII, 2, 1, 15), and one prays to the gods to
be kept from the "bonds of Nirrti" (*A.V.* I, 31, 2), as one also
implores Varuna to save one from his "bonds". Just as, in certain
cases, Agni, Soma or Rudra are invoked to deliver one from the
"bonds of Varuna", so Indra is supposed to be able to free one not
only from those bonds of Varuna, but also from the "bondage"
of the demons of death (e.g., *A.V.* IX, 3, 2-3, where it is a case of
severing the bonds of the demon Visvavāra by the help of Indra,
etc.). Illnesses are the "snares" and death is only the supreme
"bondage". This explains why these attributes, in the case of
Yama and Nirrti, are not only important, but really constitutive.

Illness and death: it is these two elements of the magico-
religious complex of "binding" which have had the widest
currency almost all over the world, and it may be worth while to
inquire whether their diffusion itself would not throw light upon

certain aspects of the problem we are considering. Before leaving India, however, let us try to summarise the most important phenomena we have observed there.

(1) Varuna, the Great Asura, magically binds culprits, and one prays to him either not to bind, or else to unbind them.

(2) Vritra imprisons the Waters, and some aspects of his myth correspond to the nocturnal, lunar and aquatic side of Varuna, in so far as these modalities of the great God express the "non-manifest" and the "blocked".

(3) Indra, like Agni and Soma, liberates men from the bonds of Varuna and from the chains of the funerary divinities; he "cuts" or "breaks" these "bonds" exactly as, in the myth, he cuts, dismembers and so on, the body of Vritra. Together with the warlike means which are proper and indeed exclusive to him, he does also employ "magical" means to triumph over the magician Vritra; but it remains true that "binding" is not one of his fundamental methods, even though the "snare" must be regarded as one of his weapons.

(4) On the contrary, bonds, cords and knots characterise the divinities of death (Yama, Nirrti) and the demons of the various maladies.

(5) And lastly, in the "popular" parts of the Vedic books, the charms against the bonds of these demons are no less numerous than the spell-binding sorceries aimed at human enemies.

We find that, even thus summarised, things are not simple. However, certain lines of force are traceable: on the mythical plane of the divine exploits, we have on the one hand the magical non-action of Varuna and of Vritra, and on the other the action of Indra; on the human plane of illness and death, there is the importance of the cords and knots among the funerary divinities and the demons, and the magical use of "binding" in popular medicine as well as in sorcery. Thus, ever since Vedic times, the "binding" complex, while it remains characteristic and constitutive of the zone of magical sovereignty, yet overflows it both upward (to the cosmological plane: Vritra) and downward (to the funerary level; Yama, Nirrti; the plane of "sorcery"). Let us see what touches we can add to this picture, after comparison with the other Indo-European domains.

THRACIANS, ANCIENT GERMANS, CAUCASIANS

It is probable, as Güntert has shown (*op. cit.*, p. 154), that the name of the Thracian god Darzales, attested by the inscriptions, is explainable from a root-word which includes the notion of "binding" (av. *darezeiti*, " to bind", *dərez*, "cord", "snare"), but we know almost nothing about this god. The same etymology is doubtless valid for the name of the Geto-Thracian god Derzélates —well known at Odessos, where they celebrated the *darzeleia* as an intercession for the harvest; and attested also at Tomis by rings that bear the inscription *Derzo*—and also for those of the Thracian-Phrygian Bendis, the Lithuanian Bentis and the Illyrian Bindus. Unfortunately very few things are known about the last two; could the human sacrifice practised by the Illyrians have been also offered to Bindus?

More revealing are certain rituals which have been preserved for us in the Teutonic tradition as much as in the Thracian-Phrygian and the Caucasian. Writing of the great annual religious festival of the Semnones, Tacitus (in *Germania*, 39) adds that those who took part in it could do so only after having been bound (*nemo nisi vinculo ligatus ingreditur*). Closs,[26] who has commented copiously on this rite and cites numerous parallels, regards it as a gesture of submission to the national deity (p. 566), whilst Pettazzoni[27] classes it rather as an ordeal. However that may be, there are grounds for comparing it with the Mithraic ceremonies of initiation, in which the neophyte's hands were bound behind his

[26] Closs, "Die Religion des Semnonenstammes" in the *Wiener Beiträge zur Kulturgeschichte und Linguistik*, IV, Salzburg-Leipzig, 1936, pp. 564 ff., 609 ff., 643, 668.

[27] R. Pettazzoni, "Regnator omnium deus" in *Studi e Materiali di Storia delle Religioni*, XIX-XX, 1943-46, pp. 142-156, p. 155.

back with a rope.[28] One remembers, too, the iron ring borne by
the Chatti "as a chain" until they had killed their first enemy
(*Germania*, 31), the ritual shackling among the Albanians (Strabon,
XI, 503); also the chains borne by the Georgian devotees of the
"White George",[29] the ritual "bindings" of the Armenian kings
(Tacitus, *Annals*, XII, 45; Closs, *op. cit.*, p. 619), and certain contemporary Albanian customs.[30] All these rites express a servile
attitude, the believer presenting himself as a slave or a prisoner
before his master. The "binding" thus takes concrete form as a
mark of vassalage.[31] Closs (*op. cit.*, 620) may be right in attributing
the ritual of the Semnones to Illyrian influence, and in thinking

[28] F. Cumont, *Les Religions orientales dans le paganisme romain*, 4th edn. Paris,
1929, plate xiii; a rope which was made *intestinis pullinis*, according to the Ps.-
Augustine, *Quaest.*, V. Cumont, *Textes et Monuments relatifs aux mystères de
Mithra*, Brussels, 1894-1900, II, pp. 7-8.

[29] Closs, *op. cit.*, p. 566; *ibid.*, p. 643, quoting O. G. Wesendonk, "Ueber
Georgisches Heidentum" in *Caucasica*, fasc. I, Leipzig, 1924, pp. 54 ff., 99, 101,
G. Dumézil, Τιτνός, in the *Rev. Hist. Relig.*, Vol. CXI, 1935, (pp. 66-
89) pp. 69 ff., studies, from Georgian sources, the "slaves of the White George":
"whoever hopes to honour or to appease the White George by becoming his
slave takes one of these chains, puts it round his neck, and thus, either walking
or kneeling, goes all round the church."

[30] During the judgment upon a vendetta, the culprit has to present himself before the "tribunal" with his hands bound. See Closs, *op. cit.*, p. 600.

[31] One has only to compare this Germano-Illyrian-Caucasian complex with the
ceremonies of "binding together by blood" (the "blood-brotherhood") which
are practised almost all over Europe, to realise the distance that separates the
bond between master and slave from the bond between the "brothers of the
cross" (the expression is Rumanian, *fratia de cruce*). Upon blood-brotherhoods,
cf. A. Dietrich, *Mutter Erde* (3rd edn. Leipzig-Berlin, 1925), p. 130 ff.; the
classic book by H. C. Trumbull, *The Blood Covenant*, London, 1887; and
Stith Thompson, *Motif-Index of Folk-Literature*, II, Helsinki, 1935, p. 125. One
may be tempted to compare these forms of brotherhood to the religious relationships between human beings and Mitra—in view of the rather stern relations between Varuna and his worshippers. Which is not at all to minimise
the religious value of Varuna—quite the reverse!

that it properly belongs to the lunar-chthonic stratum centred in
the regions of the South.[32] But apart from this ritual, we find
other elements among the ancient Germans belonging to the same
"binding" complex: for instance, the ritual death by hanging
explains the epithet applied to Odin, "god of the rope" (*Haptagud*,
Closs, p. 609); similarly, the Germanic funerary goddesses pull
up the dead with a rope,[33] and the warrior goddesses (*Disir* in
old Scandinavian, *Idisi* in old High German) bind those whom they
mean to make fall.[34] These are features to remember; they remind us of the means used by Yama and Nirrti; and they will be
made clearer by some facts we shall cite presently.

IRAN

The Iranian data are of two kinds: (1) some allusions to the demon
Astōvidhōtush, who ties up the man destined to death;[35] (2) the
conduct of the Iranian warrior-gods and heroes—Frēdūn, for
instance, ties up the demon Azdahāk and chains him to the
mountain Dimāvand (Dinkard, IX, 21, 103); the god Tistrya
binds the Pairika sorceresses with two or three ropes (*Yast*, 8, 55);
Verethragna, as we saw, binds the arms of his adversary (*Yast*, 14,

[32] A. Closs, *op. cit.*, pp. 643, 668. According to the same author (p. 567), the
binding of the ritual victim was a complex from the megalithic cultures and
from South-east Asia.

[33] J. Grimm, *Deutsche Mythologie*, II, 705, IV, 254; Scheftelowitz, *op. cit.*, p. 7.

[34] R. H. Meyer, *Altgermanische Religionsgeschichte*, 1910, pp. 158, 160. But the
personality of these goddesses is more complex; cf. Jan de Vries, *Altgermanische
Religionsgeschichte*, II, Berlin, 1937, pp. 375 ff.

[35] He binds the dying with his "bonds of death", *Yasna* 53, 8; Scheftelowitz,
Die altpersische Religion, p. 92. "It is Astōvidhōtush who binds him, and Vayu
who carries him away bound", *Vendidad*, 5, 8; H. S. Nyberg, "Questions de
cosmogonie et de cosmologie mazdéennes" II, in the *Journal Asiatique* (Oct.-
Dec. 1931, pp. 193-244), p. 205; G. Dumézil, *Tarpeia*, Paris, 1947, p. 73. Cf.
Mēnōkē Khrat 2, 115; G. Widengren, *Hochgottglaube im Alten Iran*, Uppsala,
1938, p. 196.

63); in certain episodes of the *Shah Nameh*, as Scheftelowitz has noted,[36] Ahriman holds a snare, and the bonds of the god of destiny are mentioned. The lack of any binding Sovereign corresponding to Varuna is not inexplicable: whether, as is generally supposed, the place of Varuna is occupied only by the supreme god Ahura Mazdāh, or whether it is also taken by the *amesa spenta Asa*, as M. Dumézil suggests (in his *Naissance d'Archanges*, pp. 82 ff., 100 ff.), in either case we have to do with entities that had been purified, moralised by the Zoroastrian reform, and to find the "magic" of Varuna in their nature would be inconceivable. The "sovereign" elements that survive in Ahura Mazdāh retain no trace of a "terrible sovereignty"; and although he is sometimes a god of destiny, that is so common a characteristic of supreme and ouranian gods that no conclusion at all can be drawn from it. But, seeing that we are almost wholly ignorant as to what was the Iranian equivalent to the Vedic Varuna before the Zoroastrian reform, it would be rash, and surely false, to conclude that the "binding" character of Varuna derived, in India, from a non-Aryan influence. Indeed, the Greek Ouranos himself *binds* his rivals and, as M. Dumézil has shown (in his *Ourános-Váruna, passim*), there is good reason to search the myth of Ouranos and the Ouranides for traces of a schema that was Indo-European. However that may be, the attested facts from Iran account for only two of the motifs that we have found in the Indian mythology—the god or the hero who binds demons; and the funerary demon who binds men before carrying them away to the bridge Cinvat. In consequence, it may be, of the Zoroastrian reform, the other two important Indian features—the "magic" of Varuna and the cosmological "bondage"—no longer appear.

[36] *Das Schlingen- und Netzmotiv*, p. 9; *Die altpersische Religion*, p. 92.

ETHNOGRAPHIC PARALLELS

It would be fruitless to formulate any general conclusion from the Indo-European data before widening our historic and cultural perspective, as we said we would, and integrating the "binding" complex with a vaster assemblage of analogous or identical symbolisms. But already we can point out several ethnographic parallels to the Indo-European group of gods and of funerary demons who "bind" the dead. The figure that comes nearest to the Iranian couple, Vayu-Astōvidhōtush, is no other than the Chinese god of the wind and of the net, Pauhi, whom we find in close relations with the serpent-goddess Nakura, which proves that he belongs to a chthonic and lunar stratum of culture.[37] As for the cords of Yama, of Nirrti and of Astōvidhōtush and the Germanic goddesses, their most exact counterparts are to be found in the region of the Pacific. Among the Aranda of Australia, the *tjimbarkna* demons tie up the souls of human beings during the night and kill them by vigorously tightening the rope.[38] In the Danger Islands the god of death, Vaerua, binds the dead with cords and drags them thus into the land of the dead.[39] In the Hervey Islands the soul of the deceased, going down into hell through a miraculous tree, perceives the net of the god Akaanga who is waiting for him, and whom he cannot escape.[40] At San

---

[37] Inone, cited by Closs, p. 643, Note 44. Cf. the legend of the two spirits, Shen-t'u and Yü-lei, who bind the souls of the dead to the floor of a cavern; C. Hentze, *Die Sakralbronzen und ihre Bedeutung in den frühchinesischen Kulturen*, Antwerp, 1941, p. 23.

[38] Carl Strehlow, *Die Aranda- und Loritja-Stämme in Zentral-Australien*, I, Frankfurt a-M., p. 11.

[39] W. Wyatt Gill, *Life in the Southern Isles*, London, 1876, pp. 181 ff.

[40] W. Wyatt Gill, *Myths and Songs from the South Pacific*. London, 1876, pp. 161 ff.; cf. also E. S. C. Handy, *Polynesian Religion*, Honolulu, 1927, p. 73. See M. Walleser, "Religiöse Anschauungen u. Gebräuche der Bewohner von Jap" in *Anthropos* VIII, 1913, pp. 607-629, pp. 612-613.

Cristobal the "Fisher of Souls", seated upon a rock, fishes for souls.[41] In the Solomon Islands it is the parents who fish for the soul of the deceased in order to put it into a box with a bodily relic (a skull, a jaw-bone, a tooth, etc.).[42] The sorcerers of the Hervey Islands possess magical traps, in which they catch the souls of those they want to destroy.[43] One meets with the same customs in other cultural zones,[44] but it is important to note how closely, in Melanesia, the god of death's habit of "fishing for" souls and "tying them" is analogous to the sorcerers' technique of murder. The similarity between the two kinds of "magic" helps to shed light on the problem of "binding".

It has been found that, among the Indo-Europeans, the symbols of snares, knots, and ropes are divisible into several distinct groups; between certain gods, heroes or demons, certain rituals and certain customs. Quite another aspect of the problem is presented in the Semitic world, where magic bonds of every kind are a divine (and demonic) power that is almost universal. There are sovereign gods, like Enlil and his wife Ninkhursag (= Ninlil), or even lunar deities like En-zu (= Sin), who have nets to catch those who are guilty of perjury.[45] But Shamash, the solar god, is

---

[41] Dr C. E. Fox, *The Threshold of the Pacific*, London, 1924, pp. 234 ff.

[42] W. G. Ivens, *The Melanesians of the S. E. Solomon Islands*, London, 1927, p. 178; for the same custom in Hawaii, see E. S. Craighill Handy, *op. cit.*, p. 92.

[43] W. Wyatt Gill, *Life in the Southern Isles*, pp. 180 ff.; *Myths and Songs . . .* p. 171.

[44] The Tungus shaman uses a lasso to bring back the fleeing soul of a patient, S. Shirokogorow, *The psycho-mental complex of the Tungus*, Shanghai-London; 1935, p. 290. The shaman, moreover, imitates the techniques of the spirits; *ibid.*, p. 178. The same cultural complex obtains among the Chukchi. On this problem, cf. also Eliade, *Le Chamanisme . . .*, Paris, 1951.

[45] L. W. King, *History of Sumer and Akkad*, London, 1910, pp. 128 ff. G. Furlani, *La religione babilonese-assira*, I, Bologna, 1928, p. 159; E. Dhorme, *Les Religions de Babylonie et d'Assyrie*, Collection "Mana" II, Paris, 1945, pp. 28, 49; E. Douglas van Buren, "Symbols of the Gods in Mesopotamian Art" in *Analecta Orientalia* 23, pp. 11-12.

also armed with snares and cords: prayers are addressed to him, too, for the liberation of those who are bound. The goddess Nisaba ties up the demons of illnesses: the demons, for their part have nooses, especially the demons of maladies; the demon of the plague is invoked by calling upon him: "In thy net, bind and annihilate the Babylonians!"[46] Bel (= Enlil) is addressed as: "Father Bel, who dost hurl thy nooses, and every noose is a hostile noose."[47] Tammuz is named "Lord of the snares",[48] but, in the myth, he himself is "bound" and prays to be saved from snares.[49] To Marduk, prayer is offered for deliverance from chains and snares, for he too is a master binder. Like Indra, he uses the noose and the cords as a divine champion, in the "heroic" manner. In the Epic of Creation, *Enuma Elis*, we can distinguish two sorts of "binding", recalling the Vedic pair, Varuna-Indra. Ea, the god of the Waters and of wisdom, does not fight "heroically" with the primordial monsters Apsū and Mummu: he "binds" them by magic incantations, to kill them afterwards (*Enuma Elis*, I, 60-74). Marduk, after the assembly of the gods has invested him with the prerogatives of absolute sovereignty which until then had belonged to the celestial god Anu (IV, 4 and 7), and after he has received from them the sceptre, the throne and the *pālu* (IV, 29), undertakes to fight the marine monster Tiamat; and this time it is indeed a heroic combat; but Marduk's capital weapon is still the "net", the "gift of his father Anu".[50]

---

[46] Scheftelowitz, *Das Schlingen- und Netzmotiv*, pp. 4 ff.

[47] M. Jastrow, *Die Religion Babyloniens und Assyriens*, Vol II, Giessen, 1912, p. 15.

[48] Scheftelowitz, *op. cit.*, p. 4.

[49] M. Witzel, "Tammuz-Liturgien und Verwandtes," Rome, 1937, *Analecta Orientalia*, 10, p. 140. Geo. Widengren, *Mesopotamian Elements in Manichæism*, Uppsala, 1946, p. 80.

[50] *Ibid.*, IV, 49. In the tablet I, 83, Marduk is the son of Ea, and whatever may be the meaning of this affiliation, it is of the essence of the magical sovereignty. (I follow the French translation of R. Labat, *Le Poème babylonien de la Création*, Paris, 1935.)

Marduk "binds" Tiamat (IV, 95), "shackles" him and takes away his life (IV, 104). Afterwards, he chains up all the gods and demons who have sided with Tiamat and, says the poem, "they were thrown into nets, remained in the meshes and were put into caves" (IV, 111-114, 117, 120). Marduk acquires sovereignty through his heroic struggle, but he also keeps the prerogatives of magical sovereignty. Taking into account also the magical values of cords, knots and snares in sorcery and in popular medicine (which we shall see later), the general impression we gain from this rapid survey of the Mesopotamian region is one of almost total confusion. The "binding" seems to be a magico-religious enchantment on an equal footing with all the other religious "forms". It would be interesting to see a specialist in the Mesopotamian religions tackle this problem, and find out whether one could reconstitute a "history" underlying this confusion.

THE MAGIC OF KNOTS

Let us now consider, as a whole, the morphology of ties and knots in the practice of magic. We could classify the most important facts under two main headings: (1) the magic "bonds" employed against human adversaries (in war or in sorcery), with the converse operation of "cutting the bonds"; and (2) beneficent knots and bonds, means of defence against wild animals, against diseases, witchcraft, demons and death. Restricting ourselves to a few examples, let us mention, in the first category, the magical snares employed against enemies (*Atharva Veda* II, 12, 2; VI, 104; VIII, 8, 6), the cord buried near the house of an enemy, or even hidden in his ship to make it capsize,[51] and finally, the knots that bring about all sorts of ills, both according to the magic of

[51] *Kauśītaki Saṃhitā*, XLVIII, 4-5; Caland, *Altindische Zauberritual*, Amsterdam, 1900, p. 167; V. Henry, *La Magie dans l'Inde antique*, Paris, 1903, p. 229; Scheftelowitz, p. 12.

antiquity[52] and to modern superstition.[53] As for the "cutting of the bonds", it appears already in the *Atharva Veda* (for instance, VI, 4, 2 ff.); and, in the same order of ideas but as a preventive, we often read in ethnographic literature that men ought not to be wearing any knot in their attire at certain critical times—childbirth, marriage or at death.[54]

In the second category we may include all the customs that attribute to knots and bonds a function of healing, of defence against demons, or of conservation of the magic and vital forces. Even in antiquity,[55] they used to bandage any diseased part of the body as a remedial measure, a method that is still quite common in the folk medicine of our own days.[56] Still more widespread is the custom of protecting oneself against illness and evil spirits by

[52] Ezechiel, XIII, 18-21; C. Fossey, *La Magie Assyrienne*, Paris, 1902, p. 83; M. Jastrow, *The Religion of Babylonia and Assyria*, Boston, 1898, pp. 280 ff., etc.

[53] W. Crooke, *The popular religion and folk-lore of Northern India*, Westminster, 1896, Vol. II, pp. 46 ff.; S. Seligman, *Der böse Blick*, Berlin, 1910, I, 262, 328 ff.; Scheftelowitz, p. 14; Frazer, *Taboo*, pp. 301 ff.; G. L. Kittredge, *Witchcraft in Old and New England*, Cambridge, Mass., 1929, pp. 201 ff. Cf. the *Handwörterbuch des deutschen Aberglaubens*, s.v. *Schlinge, Netz*, etc.; in folk-lore, Stith Thompson, *Motif-index*, Vol. II, p. 313.

[54] Everything has to be kept open and untied in order to facilitate childbirth, Frazer, *op. cit.*, pp. 296 ff.; but cf. the net as a defence against demons during childbirth, among the Kalmuks, Frazer, *Folk-lore in the Old Testament* III, London, 1919, p. 473. The consummation of a marriage could be prevented by the magic of cords and knots, Frazer, *Taboo*, pp. 299 ff. One cannot die as long as anything is locked or bolted in the house, *ibid.*, p. 309; and in some places they undo the ties of the shroud to ensure the repose of the soul, *ibid.*, p. 310. On the other hand, the widows in New Guinea, in order to protect themselves against the souls of the deceased, wear nets as a sign of mourning, Frazer, *The Belief in Immortality* I, London, 1913, pp. 241, 249, 260, 274, 293. It is always as a defence against the ghosts of the dead that corpses are bound, although the meaning of the custom may be more complex.

[55] *Kausitaki-Sam.*, XXXII, 3; Caland, *Altindische Zauberritual*, p. 104; R. C. Thompson, *Semitic Magic, its origins and development*, London, 1908, pp. 165 ff.

[56] Scheftelowitz, p. 29, Note 1; Frazer, *Taboo*, p. 301 ff.

means of knots, strings and cords,[57] especially during a time of childbirth.[58] Here and there all over the world, knots are worn by way of amulets.[59] It is significant that knots and strings are used in the nuptial rites to protect the young couple,[60] though at the same time, as we know, knots are thought to imperil the consummation of the marriage. But *ambivalence of this sort is to be found in all the magico-religious uses of knots and bonds*. The knots bring about illness, but also cure or drive it away; nets and knots can bewitch one, but also protect one against bewitchment; they can both hinder childbirth and facilitate it; they preserve the newly born, and make them ill; they bring death, and keep it at bay. On the whole, what is essential in all these magical and magico-medical rites, is the orientation that they give to the power that resides in any kind of binding, in every act of "tying". And this *orientation* may be either *positive* or *negative*, according to whether one takes the opposites in the sense of "benefic" or "malefic", or in that of "defence" or "attack".

MAGIC AND RELIGION

All these beliefs and all these rites certainly lead us into the domain of the *magical* mentality. Yet, from the fact that these popular practices derive from magic, have we the right to regard the general symbolism of "tying" as exclusively a creation of the magical mentality? I think not. Even if, among the Indo-Europeans, the rites and symbols of "binding" include chthonic and lunar elements, and therefore betray strong magical influences—which is not certain—we still have to explain other documents which not only express authentic religious experience but also a general conception of man and of the world which is, in

[57] In Assyria, Thompson, *op. cit.*, p. 171; Furlani, *La religione babilonese-assira*, II, Bologna, 1929, p. 166; China, India, Scheftelowitz, p. 38.
[58] India: W. Crooke, *op. cit.*, II, p. 36; Todas, etc. Scheftelowitz, p. 39.
[59] Frazer, *Taboo*, pp. 308 ff.; Scheftelowitz, p. 41.
[60] Scheftelowitz, pp. 52 ff.

itself, truly *religious* and not magical. The Mesopotamian data
that we have already passed in review, for instance, cannot be
altogether reduced to a magical interpretation. Among the
Hebrews things are still more clear: it is true that the Bible
mentions the "cords of death" in, for instance, "the cords of
Sheol entangled me, the snares of death confronted me" (II
Samuel, 22, 6, quoting *Psalms*, 18, 5) and again in "the snares of
death encompassed me, the pangs of Sheol laid hold of me; I
suffered distress and anguish. Then I called on the name of the
Lord: O Lord, I beseech thee, save my life!" (*Psalm* 116, 3-4.)
But the terrible Lord of these snares is Jahveh himself, and the
prophets depict him with nets in his hand to punish the guilty:
"As they go, I will spread over them my net; I will bring them
down like the birds of the air" (*Hosea*, 7, 12); "And I will spread
my net over him, and he shall be taken in my snare, and I will
bring him to Babylon" (*Ezechiel*, 12, 13; cf. 17, 20): "I will throw
my net over you . . . and I will haul you up in my dragnet"
(*ibid.*, 32, 3). The profound and authentic religious experience of
Job, too, discovers the same image to express the omnipotence of
God: "Know then, that God has put me in the wrong, and closed
his net about me" (*Job*, 19, 6). The Judæo-Christians, who thought
it was the devil that "bound" the infirm and diseased (as in *Luke*,
13, 16), nevertheless spoke of the most High God as "master of
the bonds". Thus we find, among the same people, a magico-
religious multivalency of "bonds"—bonds of death, of illness, of
sorcery, and also the bonds of God.[61] "A net is spread over all
living beings," wrote Rabbi Aqiba[62]—a felicitous expression, for
the vision of life it implies is neither exclusively "magical" nor
"religious", but the very situation of man in the world, in all its
complexity; to use a terminology now in fashion, it expresses the
existential condition.

[61] Consequently, we are entitled to suppose that certain Vedic allusions to the
bonds of Varuna are also expressions of a religious experience comparable to
that of Job.

[62] *Pirqē Abōt*, 3, 20; Scheftelowitz, p. 11.

In many countries the "thread of life" symbolises human destiny. "The thread of their life [literally, the cord of their tent] is broken!" cries Job (4, 21; cf. 7, 6). Achilles, like all mortals, must "suffer whatever fate may have spun for him with the linen in which his mother bore him" (*Iliad*, 20, 128; cf. 24, 210). The goddesses of fate spin the thread of human life: "There will we leave him to suffer the fate that the sad Spinsters wound on their spindle in the hour when he came out of his mother into the light . . ." (*Odyssey* 7, 198).[63] And there is more to be said of this: the cosmos itself is conceived as a tissue, as a vast "web". In Indian speculation, for instance, the air (*vāyu*) has "woven" the Universe by linking together this world and the other world and all beings, as it were by a thread (*Brihadāranyaka Upanishad*, III, 7, 2), just as the breath (*prāna*) has "woven" human life. ("Who has woven the breath within him?" asks the *Atharva Veda*, X, 2, 13.) From all this rather involved symbolism two essential things emerge: first, that in the Cosmos as well as in human life, everything is connected with everything else in an invisible web; and secondly, that certain divinities[64] are the mistresses of these "threads" which constitute, ultimately, a vast cosmic "bondage".

It is rarely that etymology yields us a decisive clue to problems as delicate as those of the "origins" of religion and magic; but it is often instructive. Scheftelowitz and Güntert have shown how in several linguistic families, the words denoting the act of "tying" serve equally well to express that of bewitching: for instance, in Turco-Tatar, *bag*, *baj*, *boj* signify both "sorcery" and "bond, cord";[65] The Greek καταδέω means to "tie strongly"

[63] Cf. *vitae fila*, Ovid, *Heroïdes*, 15, 82. See the chapter on lunar rituals and myths in my *Patterns of Comparative Religion*, pp. 154 ff.

[64] For the most part—but not always—lunar divinities, sometimes chthonico-lunar.

[65] H. Vambéry, *Die Primitive Kultur des turko-tatarischen Volkes*, Leipzig, 1879, p. 246. The notion of freeing from sorcery is conveyed by the expression "to free from the ties": among the Yoruba the word *edi*, "binding", also has the

and also to "bind by a magic charm, by tying a knot" (whence
κατάδεσμος, "cord", "to bewitch"; *Inscr. Graec.* III, 3, p. v;
Scheftelowitz, p. 17). The Latin *fascinum*, "charm, malefic spell"
is related to *fascia*, "band, bandage", and to *fascis*, "bundle";
ligāre, "to tie", and *ligātūra*, "act of tying" also mean "to charm"
and "charm" (cf. the Rumanian *legatura*, "act of tying" and "to
bewitch"). The Sanskrit *yukti*, properly "to harness", "to attach",
acquires the sense of "magic means", and the powers of Yoga are
sometimes understood as a bewitchment through "binding".[66]
All this etymology confirms the idea that the act of binding is
essentially magical. What we have here is an extreme "specialisation": to bewitch, to bind by magic, to fascinate, etc. Etymologically, *religio* also denotes a form of "attachment" to the
divinity; but it would be imprudent to understand *religio* (as
Güntert does on p. 140) in the sense of "sorcery". For, as we have
said, religion as well as magic comprises in its very essence the
element of "binding", although, of course, with a different
intensity and, above all, a contrary orientation.

THE SYMBOLISM OF "LIMIT-SITUATIONS"

There are several other symbolical complexes that are characteristic, in almost the same formulas, of the structure of the Cosmos
and the "situation" of man in the world. The Babylonian word
markasu "link, cord", means, in the mythology, "the cosmic
principle that unites all things", and also "the support, the power

---

meaning of magic, and the Ewe word *vōsesa*, "amulet", means "untied"; see
A. B. Ellis, *Yoruba-speaking peoples*, London, 1894, p. 118.

[66] For example, *Mahābhārata*, XIII, 41, 3 ff., where Vipulā "had subdued the
senses (of Ruci) by means of the bonds of Yoga"; see Eliade, *Yoga, Immortality
and Freedom*, p. 18. Also Ananda K. Coomaraswamy, "Spiritual Paternity"
and "the Puppet-Complex" in *Psychiatry*, VIII, No. 3, August 1945, pp. 25-35,
esp. pp. 29 ff.

and the divine law that hold the universe together".[67] Similarly
Tchuang-tzü (Chap. VI) speaks of the *Tao* as "the chain of the
entire creation",[68] reminding us of the Indian cosmological
terminology. On the other hand, the labyrinth is sometimes conceived as a "knot" which has to be "un-tied", and this notion
belongs to a metaphysico-ritual unity which comprises the ideas of
difficulty, of danger, of death and of initiation.[69] Upon another
plane, that of knowledge and wisdom, one meets with similar
expressions: people speak of "deliverance" from illusions (which,
in India, bear the same name as the magic of Varuna, *māyā*); they
seek to "tear away" the veils of unreality, to "untie" the "knots"
of existence, etc. This gives one the impression that the situation
of man in the world, in whatever perspective it may be viewed,
is always expressed by key-words conveying the ideas of "bond-

[67] S. Langdon, *Semitic Mythology*, Boston, 1931, p. 109. Several Babylonian
temples are named *markas shamē u irshiti*, "the Link between Heaven and Earth",
cf. E. Burrows, "Some cosmological patterns in Babylonian religion" in the
volume *Labyrinth*, edited by S. H. Hook, London, 1935 (pp. 45-70) pp. 47-48,
n.2. An ancient Sumerian name for the temple is "the *dimgal* of the region";
Burrows, (p. 47, Note 7) proposes to translate this "Great binding post"; *dim*
meaning "post", etc. and also "rope"; Probably *dim* = "to bind, thing to bind
to or to bind with". The symbolism of "binding" would here be integrated into
a greater whole which might be called the "Symbolism of the Centre" (see
above, pp. 41ff.).

[68] "The link of all Creation" in Hughes's translation in *Everyman's Library*,
p. 193). The character translated by "link" is *hsi* (Giles, 4062), which means
"dependence, fastening, link, tie, nexus, chain, lineage, etc. Cf. A. K. Coomaraswamy, "The iconography of Dürer's 'Knots' and of Leonardo's 'concatena-
tion'" in the *Art Quarterly*, Spring 1944, pp. 109-128, Note 19.

[69] Cf. the labyrinths in the form of knots, in the funerary rituals and beliefs at
Malekula; A. Bernard Deacon, "Geometrical drawings from Malekula and
other Islands of the New Hebrides" in the *Journal of the Anthropological Institute*,
Vol. LXVI, 1934, pp. 129-175; and the same author's *Malekula, a vanishing
people of the New Hebrides*, London, 1934, esp. pp. 552 ff.; John Layard, "Toten-
fahrt auf Malekula" in the *Eranos Jahrbuch*, 1937, Zürich, 1938, pp. 242-291;
and *Stone Men of Malekula*, London, 1942, pp. 340 ff., 649 ff.

age, shackling, attachment", etc. On the magical plane, a man makes use of amulets of knots to protect himself against the binding spells of the demons and sorcerers; and, on the religious plane, he feels that he is "bound" by God, caught in his "snare"; but death also "binds" him, either concretely (the corpse is "tied up") or metaphorically (the demons "bind" the soul of the deceased). Nay, more—life itself is a "web" (sometimes a magic web of cosmic proportions, *māyā*) or a "thread" on which every mortal life is strung. These various views have certain points in common; in all of them the end and aim of man is to free himself from "bonds". To the mystical initiation of the labyrinth—in the course of which one learns to undo the labyrinthine knot in order to be able to do so when the soul meets with it after death—to this corresponds the philosophic, metaphysical initiation, undertaken to "rend the veil" of ignorance and liberate the soul from the shackles of existence. We know how Indian thought is dominated by the thirst for liberation, and how its most characteristic terminology is all reducible to antithetic formulas such as "chained-liberated", "bound-unbound", "attachment-detachment", etc.[70] The same formulas were current in Greek philosophy; in the cave of Plato, the men are bound by chains which prevent their moving or turning their heads (*Republic*, VII, 514 *et seq.*). The soul, "after its fall, has been captured, it is in chains . . .; it is said to be in a tomb, and in a cave, yet, by turning again towards ideas, it frees itself from its bonds . . ."

This multivalency of the "binding" complex—which we have now observed on the planes of cosmology, magic, religion, initiation, metaphysics and soteriology—is probably due to man's *recognising, in this complex, a sort of archetype of his own situation in the world.* In doing so, he helps to raise a problem in anthropology, a properly philosophical study of which stands to gain much by

[70] See my *Yoga, Immortality and Freedom, passim*. In his article on "The iconography of Dürer's 'knots' . . .", A. K. Coomaraswamy has studied the metaphysical values of knots and their survival in popular art, as well as among certain artists of the Middle Ages and the Renaissance.

taking account of these documents about certain "limit-situations" of archaic man. For, although contemporary thought
prides itself upon having rediscovered the concrete man, it is no
less true that its analyses refer mainly to the condition of modern
Western man, so that it is biased by its lack of universality, by a
kind of "provincialism" tending, in the end, to monotony and
sterility.

The "binding" complex raises, moreover, or rather it constitutes, a problem which is of the highest interest to the historian
of religions; not only because of the relations it reveals between
magic and religion, but above all because it shows us what may
be called the proliferation of magico-religious forms and the
"physiology" of these forms; we can feel the presence of an
archetype of "binding" which is trying to realise itself upon the
different planes of magico-religious life (cosmology, mythology,
sorcery, etc.) as well as at the different levels of each of these
planes (great magic and little magic, for instance, aggressive
sorcery and defensive sorcery). In one sense, we might even say
that, *as the "terrible sovereign", either historic or historicised, is striving
to imitate his divine prototype, the "binding" god, so every sorcerer, too,
is imitating the terrible sovereign and his divine prototype.* Morphologically, too, there is no break in continuity between Vritra who
"chains up" the Waters, Varuna who "binds" the guilty, the
demons who catch the dead in their "net" and the sorcerers who
bind the enemy by magic, or unbind the victims of other
sorcerers. All these operations are of the same structure. In the
present state of our knowledge, it is difficult to specify whether
their uniformity proceeds from imitation—from "historic"
borrowings, in the sense given to this term by the historico-
cultural school—or whether it is to be explained by the fact that
they all follow from *the very situation of man in the world*—so that
they are variants of one and the same archetype realising itself on
many planes and in different cultural areas. It seems indubitable,
at least in the case of certain patterns such as that of Indo-European
magic sovereignty, that we are dealing with mythico-ritual

complexes of a *historical* solidarity. But the historicity of the Indo-European "binding" complex does not necessarily imply that all the other magico-religious customs and beliefs all over the world related to a similar complex must also be "historical"—that is, derived from one and the same ancestral origin by direct or indirect influences, borrowings, etc. Let us add that, if the Indo-European case does not necessarily imply this conclusion, neither does it exclude it. The question must be left open.

SYMBOLISM AND HISTORY

But by way of comparison, we might cite an analogous case: the complex of ritual ascension and the magical flight. Though we can discern certain historical relations (filiation, borrowings) between the different beliefs and systems (rituals, mysticisms, etc.) which include ascension as one of their essential elements,[71] the morphology of ascension and of the symbolism of flight far surpasses these historic connections. Even should we succeed, some day, in identifying *the* historic source from which all the rituals and symbolisms of ascension emanated; even were we therefore to find ourselves in a position to specify the mechanism and the stages of their diffusion, much would still remain to be explained —the symbolism of the dream of ascension, of waking dreams and æsthetic visions, which are not only centred in the complex of ascension and flight, but present this complex already organised, and charged with the same values that are revealed in the rituals, the myths and *philosophumena* of ascension. I have sketched the outlines of such a comparative study elsewhere.[72] Here, let us be content with the conclusion that we have to do with non-historical expressions of the same archetypal symbolism, manifesting itself in a coherent and systematic manner on the plane of the

[71] See Eliade, *Le Chamanisme et les techniques archaïques de l'extase*, pp. 137 ff., 296 ff., 362 ff., 423 ff. and *passim*.

[72] Cf. Eliade, *Myths, Dreams and Mysteries*, pp. 99 ff.

"unconscious" (of dream, hallucination or waking dream) as well as upon those of the "trans-conscious" and the conscious (æsthetic vision, ritual, mythology and *philosophumena*). And let us emphasise, by the way, that the manifestations of the unconscious and the subconscious present values, and a structure, that are in perfect agreement with those of the conscious manifestations; and that, since the latter are "reasonable", in the sense that their values are logically justifiable, we might speak of a sub- or trans-conscious "logic" which is not always heterogeneous to "normal" logic (meaning thereby classical logic, or that of good sense). Provisionally, then, let us accept the hypothesis that at least a certain zone of the subconscious is ruled by the archetypes which also dominate and organise conscious and transconscious experience. Hence we are entitled to regard the multiple variants of the same complexes of symbols (such as those of "ascension" and of "binding") as endless successions of "forms" which, on the different levels of dream, myth, ritual, theology, mysticism, metaphysics, etc., are trying to "realise" the archetype.

These "forms", it is true, are not all spontaneous; not all of them depend directly upon the ideal archetype; a great many of them are "historical" in the sense that they result from the evolution or the imitation of a previously existing form. Certain variants of "binding" by sorcery are rather disconcertingly simian in this respect. They give one the impression of having been copied, on their own limited plane, from pre-existent "historical forms" of magical sovereignty or funerary mythology. But here we must be careful, for it is very commonly the case that pathological variants of religious complexes also have a superficially simian appearance. What seems more reliable is the tendency of every "historical form" to approximate as nearly as possible to its archetype, even when it has been realised at a secondary or insignificant level: this can be verified everywhere in the religious history of humanity. Any local goddess tends to become *the* Great Goddess; any village anywhere *is* the "Centre of the World", and any wizard whatever pretends, at the height

of his ritual, to be the Universal Sovereign. It is this same tendency towards the archetype, towards the restoration of the
perfect form—of which any myth or rite or divinity is only a
variant, and often rather a pale one—that makes the history of
religions possible. Without this, magico-religious experience
would be continually creating transitory or evanescent forms of
gods, myths, dogmas, etc.; and the student would be faced by a
proliferation of ever new types impossible to set in order. But
when once it is "realised"—"historicised"—the religious form
tends to disengage itself from its conditions in time and space and
to become universal, to return to the archetype. And, finally, the
"imperialism" of the victorious religious forms is also explainable by this tendency of every hierophany or theophany to
become *everything*—that is, to sum up in itself all manifestations
of the holy, to incorporate all the immense morphology of the
sacred.[72]

Whatever one may think of these general views, it is probable
that the magico-religious complex of "binding" corresponds
closely to an archetype, or constellation of archetypes (several of
which we have noted—the weaving of the Cosmos, the thread of
human destiny, the labyrinth, the chain of existence, etc.). The
ambivalence and heterogeneity of the motives of "binding" and
of "knots", and also of "deliverance from bonds", show once
again how multiple and various are the planes on which these
archetypes have been "realised". This is not, of course, to say that
amidst this enormous mass of data relating to the magico-
religious facts in question one cannot distinguish certain groups
that are *historically interconnected*, or that we have no right to regard them as dependent upon one another, or as all derived from a
common source. That is what Güntert, Dumézil and A. Closs
have done, from different points of view, in the Indo-European
field. But one hesitates to follow Closs when, faithful to the
principles of the historico-cultural school of Vienna,[74] he ventures

[73] See Eliade, *Patterns in Comparative Religion*, pp. 459 ff.
[74] The historico-cultural school of W. Schmidt and W. Koppers has hitherto

to explain this or that rite or myth of "binding", in America or Melanesia, as historically dependent upon the same source as the Indo-European forms. More plausible is his hypothesis of the Caucasian origin (p. 643) of the Indo-European ritual complex of "binding": the Finno-Ugrians and the Turko-Tatars know nothing of rites and myths of "binding", which does seem to indicate that the origin of this complex must be looked for in the countries of the South. Indeed, the nearest parallels to the Georgian rite of the chains (that of "White George" mentioned above) are to be found in India: on the one hand, there is the iron ring that the sorcerer (Panda) of the Gonds[75] wears round his neck during the nine days of the feast of Kālī-Dūrga (a festival that the Gonds call *zvārā*, a word derived from the Hindu *javārā*, "oats", a proof of its agrarian origin); and, on the other hand, there are the rings of iron about the necks of a feminine idol and of the "proto-Shiva", both found at Mohenjo-Daro.[76] It would, of course, be rash to assume that the present rite of the Gonds is directly derived from the proto-historic culture of the Indus, but the correspondences that W. Koppers establishes between these facts are not without interest.[77]

---

rendered important services to the history of religions, but its theses, carried to extremes, end in such a historicising of man as practically to eliminate all spiritual spontaneity. Though we cannot conceive man as other than a historical being, it is no less true that by his very nature man opposes himself to history, strives to abolish it and to rediscover, by every means, a timeless "paradise" in which his situation would be not so much a "historical situation" as an "anthropological" one (see my book *The Myth of the Eternal Return*).

[75] Cf. W. Koppers, "Zentralindische Fruchtbarkeitsriten und ihre Beziehungen zur Induskultur" in the *Geographica Helvetica*, I, 1946, Heft 2, pp. 165-177, pp. 168 ff.

[76] Cf. J. Marshall, *Mohenjo-Daro and the Indus Civilization*, London, 1931, Vol. I, plate xii, 8, 17.

[77] As for the ritual function of knots in the Ægean religions (see Arthur Evans's *The Palace of Minos*, I, pp. 430 ff.), it is not yet understood. Denied by

However, the frequency of the motifs of "binding" and of "knots" in the archaic strata of the Mesopotamian religions remains still to be explained. Can this be a lateral variant which (in contrast to what happened among the Indo-Europeans) was unable to organise itself into a theological and ritual system and impose itself upon the religious life as a whole; a variant which then became multiplied to infinity, and was transformed into a divine as well as a demonic magic, annexed by every divinity and exploited by every sorcerer? What we do know is that it is only among Indo-Europeans that the "binding" complex is found organically integrated into the very structure of "terrible" sovereignty, both divine and human; and that it is only among Indo-Europeans—as M. Dumézil's researches especially have shown—that we find a *coherent system*, and one that is generally applicable at the levels of ritual, mythology, theology, etc. And yet—as the preceding pages have tried to show—this *system*, centred in the conception of the Terrible Sovereign, did not exhaust the creative power in the magico-religious forms and symbolisms relative to "binding"; and of that fact we have even tried to find an explanation upon the planes of magic, mythology and of religion itself. It may be due to the very situation of man in the world (spontaneous "origin"), or to more or less servile imitation of already existing forms (historical "genesis"). But whichever explanation one prefers, the complexity of the Indo-European conception of the sovereign and terrible god is henceforth certain. We begin to glimpse the prehistory of it, we are prepared to discern traces of foreign religious traditions. It would perhaps be incorrect to define this conception as an exclusively magical one, although its structure often invites us so to regard it. On the one

---

M. P. Nilsson, who reduces it to a merely decorative value (*Minoan Mycenæan Religion*, Lund, 1927, pp. 137 ff., 349 ff.), this ritual function has lately been confirmed by Axel W. Persson, in *The Religion of Greece in Prehistoric Times*, Berkeley and Los Angeles, 1942, pp. 38 and 68. Cf. also Charles Picard, *Les Religions préhelléniques. Crète et Mycènes*, Paris, 1948, pp. 194-195.

hand, in India itself, we have underlined the cosmogonic and metaphysical values of the "bindings" of Varuna and Vritra, and, on the other hand, the religious experiences induced by this same complex among the Hebrews prove that a very pure and profound religious life may find nourishment even in "bondage" to a God of terrible and "binding" appearance.

IV

Observations on the
Symbolism of Shells

THE MOON AND THE WATERS

Oysters, sea-shells, the snail and the pearl figure constantly in aquatic cosmology as well as in sexual symbolism. They all participate, indeed, in the sacred powers which are concentrated in the Waters, in the Moon and in Woman; they are, moreover, emblems of these forces for a variety of reasons—the resemblance between the marine shell and the genital organs of woman, the relations between oysters, waters and the moon, and, lastly, the gynæcological and embryological symbolism of the pearl formed within the oyster. Belief in the magical virtues of oysters and of shells is to be found all over the world, from prehistoric until modern times.[1] The symbolism that lies at the origin of such

[1] G. F. Kunz and Charles Hugh Stevenson, *The Book of the Pearl*, London, 1908, have collected considerable documentary material about the distribution of pearls. J. W. Jackson's "The geographical distribution of the use of Pearls and Pearl-shells", a memoir republished in the volume *Shells as Evidence of the Migration of Early Culture*, Manchester, 1917, complements the information of Kunz and Stevenson. One can find what is essential in the enormous bibliography upon the magic function of shells, in the article by W. L. Hildbergh, "Cowrie-shells as Amulets in Europe" in *Folk-Lore*, Vol. 53-54, 1942-43, pp. 178-195. Cf. also the various contributions to the same problem published in the review *Man*, October, 1939, No. 165, p. 167 (M. A. Murray, "The Meaning of the Cowrie-shell", thinks that the magical value of the cowrie comes from its resemblance to a half-closed eye); Jan. 1940, No. 20 (Murray replying to Sheppard); No. 61, pp. 50-53 (Dr Kurt Singer, "Cowrie and Baubo in early Japan" publishes a neolithic Japanese statuette demonstrating the assimilation

conceptions very probably belongs to a deep level of "primitive" thinking. But it has known various "activations" and interpretations: we find oysters and shells in agricultural, nuptial or funerary rites, in the ornamentation of clothing, and in certain decorative motifs, even though, in some cases, their magico-religious meanings seem to have been half lost or debased. Among certain peoples shells still furnish decorative motifs when their magical valency is no longer even a memory. The pearl, once an emblem of the generative powers or a symbol of a transcendent reality, has retained only the value of a "precious stone" in the Western world. The steady degradation of the symbolism will be more clearly apparent at the end of our exposition.

The iconographic conjunction of Water with oysters is abundantly attested in pre-Columbian America. The "Tula relief" of Malinche Hill represents a divinity surrounded with Waters containing oysters, spirals and double circles.[2] In the *Codex Nuttall* the iconographic complex Water-Fish-Serpent-Crab-Oyster is predominant.[3] The *Codex Dresdensis* depicts Water sometimes flowing from oyster shells, sometimes filling vases formed by coiled serpents.[4] The Mexican god of the storm wore a chain of gold with little marine shells hanging from it;[5]

---

of the shell to the vulva); No. 78, (C. K. Meek, "Cowrie in Nigeria"); No. 79 (M. D. W. Jeffreys, "Cowrie shells in British Cameroon" is against Miss Murray's hypothesis); No. 101 (Balkans), No. 102 (J. H. Huttons, Naga Hills), No. 187 (Grigson, Central Provinces, India); 1941, No. 36 (C. K. Meek, Nigeria); No. 37 (Fiji, Egypt, Saxons); 1942; No. 71 (M. D. W. Jeffreys, "Cowrie, Vulva, Eye").

[2] Peñafiel, *Monumentos del arte mexicano antiguo*, p. 154, reproduced by Leo Wiener, *Mayan and Mexican Origins*, Cambridge, 1926, Pl. iv, fig. 8.

[3] Wiener, *ibid.*, Pl. iv, fig. 13; Pl. vii, fig. 14, reproducing the *Codex Nuttall*, pp. 16, 36, 43, 49.

[4] *Codex Dresdensis*, p. 34, etc., reproduced by Wiener, fig. 112-116.

[5] B. de Sahagun, *Historia general de las cosas de Nueva España*, Mexico, 1896, Vol. I, Chap. 5; Wiener, p. 68, cf. fig. 75.

and the symbol of the god of the moon was a great sea snail.[6]

In ancient China the symbolism of the oyster is even better preserved; there, the shells participate in the sacredness of the Moon, and at the same time they embody those of the aquatic powers. In the treatise *Lū shī ch'un ts'iu* of the third century B.C., we read: "The moon is the root of all that is *yin*; when the moon is full, the *pang* and the *ko* mussels are full; all *yin* things are abundant (waxing); when the moon is dark (the last day of the moon) the *pang* and *ko* mussels are empty: all *yin* things are deficient (waning)."[7] Mo-tsī, of the fifth century B.C., after having observed that the pearl oyster *pang* is born without help of the male, adds: "Therefore, that the *pang* can at length bear the pearl is because it concentrates wholly on its *yin* force."[8] "The moon," writes Liu Ngan of the second century B.C., "is the origin of *yin*. That is why the brains of fish shrink when the moon is empty, and why the shells of univalves are not full of fleshy parts when the moon is dead." The same author adds, in another chapter: "The bivalves, the crabs, the pearls and the turtles grow and diminish with the moon."[9]

Yin represents, among other things, the feminine energy of the cosmos, lunar and "humid". Any excess of *yin* activity in a particular region exasperates the feminine sexual instinct and causes "lascivious women to pervert the men" (*I Chou shu*, chap. 54, quoted by Karlgren, *op. cit.*, p. 38). There is indeed a mystical correspondence between the two principles *yin* and *yang* and

[6] J. W. Jackson, "The Aztec Moon-cult and its relation to the Chank-cult of India", *Manchester Memoirs*, Manchester, 1916, Vol. 60, No. 5, p. 2.

[7] See B. Karlgren, "Some fecundity symbols in ancient China" in the *Bulletin of the Museum of Far Eastern Antiquities*, No. 2, Stockholm, 1930, pp. 1–54, p. 36.

[8] See B. Karlgren, *ibid.*: cf. the relations between pearls, shell-fish and the Moon in Granet, *Danses et Légendes de la Chine ancienne*, Paris, 1926, pp. 480, 514, etc.

[9] J.-J. de Groot, *Les fêtes annuellement célébrées à Émouï. Étude concernant la religion populaire des Chinois*, Paris, 1886, Vol. II, p. 491. Relations between the moon and water, *ibid.*, pp. 488 ff. Influence of the moon upon pearls, pp. 490 ff.

human society. The king's chariot was ornamented with jade (rich in *yang*), and that of the queen with peacock feathers and shell-work, emblems of *yin*. The rhythms of cosmic life pursue their normal course so long as the circulation of these opposite and complementary principles is proceeding without hindrance. Sün-tzĭ writes: "If there is jade in the mountain its trees will be flourishing (rich, well-nourished); if the deep water produces pearls, the vegetation of the banks will not wither" (Karlgren, *ibid.* p. 40). We shall see, later on, that the same symbolic polarity, jade and pearl, reappears in Chinese funerary customs.

Concerning the influence of the phases of the moon upon oysters, analogous ideas were known to antiquity. Lucilius writes: *Luna alit ostrea et implet echinos, muribus fibras et jecur addit*: "The moon nourishes the oysters, fills out the sea-urchins, gives strength and vigour to the mussels" (Pliny, *Hist. Nat.*, II, 41, 3). Aulus Gellius (in his *Noctes Atticæ*, XX, 8) claims, as do several other writers, to have observed similar phenomena. This para-scientific tradition, inherited from an ancient symbolism whose meaning was no longer understood, was destined to survive in Europe up to the eighteenth century.[10]

THE SYMBOLISM OF FECUNDITY

Probably even more than the aquatic origin and the lunar symbolism attaching to oysters and sea-shells, their likeness to the vulva helped to spread belief in their magical virtues.[11] The analogy is, moreover, sometimes described in the very same terms that denote certain bivalve molluscs, as, for instance, the old

[10] P. Saintyves, *L'Astrologie populaire, étudiée spécialement dans les doctrines et les traditions relatives à l'influence de la lune*, Paris, 1937, pp. 231 ff.
[11] See Aigremont, "Muschel und Schecke als Symbol der Vulva einst und jetzt" in *Anthropophyteia*, 1909, VI, pp. 35-40; J. J. Meyer, *Trilogie altindischer Mächte und Feste der Vegetation*, Zürich, 1937, Vol. I, p. 233. See also the review *Man*, 1939-1942.

Danish word for "oyster", *kudefisk* (*kude*=vulva; cf. Karlgren, p. 34, note). Homology between the shell and the female genital organ is also attested in Japan.[12] The marine shell and the oyster participate in this way in the magical powers of the womb. In them are presented and deployed the creative forces that emanate from every emblem of the feminine principle, as from an inexhaustible source. Thus, worn upon the skin as an amulet or ornament, oysters, sea-shells and pearls endue woman with an energy propitious to fecundity, whilst also protecting her from harmful forces and ill-fortune. The Akamba women wear girdles decorated with oyster shells, which they cease to wear after the birth of their first child.[13] Elsewhere, oysters are considered the most appropriate of wedding presents. In Southern India the girls wear necklaces of marine shells,[14] and modern Hindu therapy makes use of powdered pearl for its invigorating and aphrodisiac

[12] Cf. Andersson, *Children of the yellow earth. Studies in prehistoric China*, London, 1934, p. 305. The female neolithic image published by Dr Kurt Singer (*Cowrie and Baubo in early Japan*) presents a monstrous vulva which is no other thing than a giant shell suspended on a cord. The bivalve shell plays a part in the myth of the rebirth of O-Kuninushi. According to Kurt Singer, this idol might represent Ama-no-Uzume-no-Mikoto "the Terrible Woman of Heaven" who dances with robe uplifted *usque ad partes privatas* (as Chamberlain expresses it) and who, by the laughter she provokes, forces the Sun-Goddess Amaterasu to come out of the cave in which she is hidden. The naturalists of the eighteenth century, also, founded their conchological classifications upon resemblances to the vulva. G. Elliot Smith, in *The Evolution of the Dragon*, Manchester, 1919, quotes the following lines from the *Histoire naturelle du Sénégal* (eighteenth century) by Adamson: "Concha Venerea sic dicta quia partem foemineam quodam modo repraesentat: externe quidem per labiorum fissuram, interne vero propter cavitatem uterum mentientem."

[13] Andersson, *Children of the yellow earth*, p. 304. See also C. K. Meek, in *Man*, 1940, No. 78.

[14] Andersson, *ibid.*, p. 304. The Tiagy young women wear the shell of a mollusc as a symbol of their virginity; upon the loss of which they must give up wearing the shell.

qualities[15]—one more "scientific" adaptation, on the concrete and immediate plane, of an archaic symbolism only half understood.

The cosmological function and the magical value of the pearl have been known since Vedic times. A hymn of the *Atharva Veda* (IV, 10) eulogises it thus: "Born of the wind, of the air, of the lightning, of the light, may the shell born from gold, the pearl, defend us from fear! With the shell born from the ocean, the first of all luminous things, we kill the demons (*raksas*) and we triumph over the devouring [demons]. With the shell [we triumph over] disease and poverty. . . . The shell is our universal remedy; the pearl preserves us from fear. Born of heaven, born of the sea, brought by the Sindhu, to us the shell born from gold is the jewel (*mani*) that lengthens life. Jewel born of the sea, sun born of the cloud, may it shield us on all sides from the arrows of the Gods and the Asuras. Thou art one of the golds ["pearl" is one of the names of gold], thou art born of the moon (*Sōma*), thou dost adorn the chariot and sparkle from the quiver. Prolong our lives! The bones of the gods are turned to pearl; they take life and move in the bosom of the waters. I put thee on for life, vigour and strength, for the life of a hundred autumns. May the pearl protect thee!"

The Chinese physician, for his part, holds that pearl is an excellent drug for its fertilising and gynæcological virtues.[16] According to a Japanese belief, certain mussels assist parturition; whence they are called "easy child-bed mussels" (Andersson, *loc. cit.*, p. 304). In China, they advise one never to give pregnant women a certain oyster which has the property of hastening delivery (Karlgren, p. 36). Oysters, since they contain the *yin*-principle only, are favourable to parturition and sometimes precipitate it. The resemblance between the pearl developing in the

[15] Kunz and Stevenson, *The Book of the Pearl*, p. 309, quoting Surindro Mohan Tagore, *Mani-Mālā or a Treatise on Gems*, Calcutta, 1881.

[16] Cf. J. W. Jackson, *Shells as evidence of the migrations of early culture*, p. 101; De Groot, *The religious system of China*, Vol. I, Leiden, 1898, pp. 217, 277.

oyster and the fœtus is also mentioned by Chinese authors. In *Pei ya* (eleventh century) it is said of the oyster *pang* that, when "gravid with the pearl", it is like (a woman) carrying the fœtus in her womb; and that is why the *pang* is called "the womb of the pearl" (Karlgren, p. 36).

Among the Greeks, the pearl was the emblem of love and of marriage.[17] Moreover, since pre-Hellenic times shell-fish had been closely connected with the Great Goddesses.[18] Shell-fish were sacred to Aphrodite in Cyprus, whither that goddess had been taken after being born from the sea foam (Pliny, *Hist. Nat.*, IX, 30; XXXII, 5). The myth of Aphrodite's birth from a marine conch was probably widespread in the Mediterranean world. Plautus, in translating a line of Diphilus, knew it by tradition: *Te ex concha natam esse autumnant.*[19] In Syria the goddess was named the "Lady of Pearls"; at Antioch, Margaritō.[20] The Aphrodite-shellfish complex is confirmed, furthermore, by numerous engravings upon shells (Déonna, *op. cit.*, p. 402). The resemblance of the marine shell to the female genital organ was doubtless known to the Greeks also. The birth of Aphrodite in a conch was an illustration of the mystical relation between the goddess and what she symbolised; and it was this symbolism of birth and of regeneration that inspired the ritual function of shells.[21] It is thanks to their creative power—as emblems of the universal matrix—that

---

[17] Kunz and Stevenson, *op. cit.*, pp. 307 ff.

[18] Cf. Charles Picard, *Les religions préhelléniques*, pp. 60, 80, etc.

[19] W. Déonna, "Aphrodite à la coquille" (in the *Revue Archéologique*, November-December 1917, (pp. 312-416), p. 309.

[20] Déonna, p. 400.

[21] Cf. *Dictionnaire des Antiquités*, s.v. *Bucina*; Forres in *Reallexicon*, s.v. Musselschmuck; Pauly-Wissova, s.v. *Margaritai*; Déonna, p. 406; G. Bellucci, *Parallèles ethnographiques*, Perugia, 1915, pp. 25-27; U. Pestallozza, "Sulla rappresentazione di un pithos arcaico-beotico" in *Studi e Materiali di Storia delle Religioni*, Vol. XIV, 1938, (pp. 12-32), pp. 14 ff. Hoernes-Menghin, *Urgeschichte der bildenden Kunst in Europa*, Vienna, 1925, p. 319, fig. 1-4 (figurines of Thracian origin, in the form of shells).

shells play their part in funerary rites. Such a symbolism of regeneration does not easily fade away; the scallop shells symbolising the resurrection on so many Roman funerary monuments passed over into Christian art (Déonna, p. 408). Often, moreover, the dead woman is identified with Venus; she is represented upon the sarcophagus with the breast bared and the dove at her feet (*ibid.*, p. 409); by thus identifying herself with the archetype of life in perpetual renewal, the deceased woman is ensuring her own resurrection.

The sea-shell, the pearl and the snail figure everywhere among the emblems of love and marriage. The statue of Kāmadeva is adorned with shell-work.[22] In India the nuptial ceremony is announced by the blowing of a great marine chank.[23] This same shell (*Turbinella pyrum*) is also one of the two principal symbols of Vishnu. Its religious valencies are illustrated in a prayer: "At the mouth of this shell is the God of the Moon, on its side is Varuna, on its back Prajāpati and on the apex the Ganges, the Saraswati and all the other sacred rivers of the three worlds in which they make ablutions according to the commands of Vāsudeva. In this chank is the chief of the Brahmans. This is why we must worship the sacred chank. Glory to thee, sacred shell, blessed by all the gods, born in the sea and formerly held by Vishnu in his hand. We adore the sacred chank and meditate upon it. May we be filled with joy!"[24]

Among the Aztecs, the snail used commonly to represent conception, pregnancy and parturition.[25] In a comment upon Plate xxvi of the *Codex Vaticanus*, Kingsborough translates the

[22] J. J. Meyer, *Trilogie altindische Mächte und Feste der Vegetation*, Zürich, 1937, Vol. I, p. 29.

[23] J. W. Jackson, "Shell-Trumpets and their distribution in the Old and the New Worlds" in *Manchester Memoirs*, 1916, No. 8, p. 7.

[24] Hornell, *The Sacred Chank of India*, Madras Fisheries Publications, 1914, quoted by Jackson, *The Aztec Moon-Cult*, pp. 2-3.

[25] Jackson, *The Aztec Moon-Cult*, *passim*.

native's explanation of the association of the mollusc (sea-snail) with childbirth: ". . . as this marine animal comes out of its shell, so is a man born from the womb of his mother."[26] There is the same autochthonous interpretation of Plate xi of the *Codex Telleriano-Remensis* (*ibid.*, VI, p. 122).

THE RITUAL FUNCTIONS OF SHELLS

By the same symbolism we can now easily account for the presence of sea-shells, of oysters and of pearls in many a religious rite, in agrarian and initiatory ceremonies. Oysters and pearls, which promise well for conception and parturition, also exert a happy influence upon the harvest. The power signified by a fertility-symbol manifests itself at all cosmic levels.

In India, the conch was blown not only during the ceremonies that took place in temples but also at agricultural, nuptial or funerary ceremonies (see the numerous references given in Jackson's *Shell-Trumpets*, p. 3). In Siam, the priests sound the shell-trumpet when the seed is first sown. On the coast of Malabar when the first-fruits are gathered, the priest comes out of the temple preceded by a man blowing a conch. The same ritual function of the shell obtains among the Aztecs: certain manuscripts represent the god of the Flowers and of Food carried in a procession headed by a priest sounding the conch.[27]

We have seen how exactly the sea-shell and the oyster express the symbolism of birth and rebirth. The initiation ceremonies include a symbolic death and resurrection: the shell can signalise the act of spiritual rebirth (resurrection) as effectually as it assures and facilitates carnal birth. Hence the rite, which, among certain Algonquin tribes, consists in striking the neophyte with a shell in the course of the initiation ceremony, and in showing him a shell whilst the cosmological myths and the traditions of the tribe are

[26] Kingsborough, *Antiquities of Mexico*, London, 1831-1848, Vol. VI, p. 203.
[27] Jackson, *The Aztec Moon-Cult*, pp. 3 and 4.

recited to him.[28] Shells hold, moreover, an important place in the religious life and the magical practices of numerous tribes in America (cf. Jackson, *Shell-Trumpets*, pp. 17 ff.). In the initiation ceremonies of the "Great-Medicine Society" of the Ojibwa and the "Medicine Rite" of the Winnebago, shells appear as an indispensable element. The ritual death and resurrection of the candidate are brought on by the touch of magic shells, kept in satchels of otter-skin.[29]

The same mystical links that connect the shells with the ceremonies of initiation and, in a more general way, with the various religious rites, are found again in Indonesia, in Melanesia and in Oceania.[30] The entrances to the villages in Togo are adorned with idols whose eyes are made of shells, and in front of them there are heaped-up offerings of shells. Shells are also offered to the rivers, to the springs and to trees. The magico-religious virtues of shells also explain their presence in the administration of justice.[31] As in Chinese society, so also in "primitive" societies, the emblem that embodies one of the cosmic principles ensures the just application of the law: inasmuch as it is a symbol of the cosmic Life, a shell has the power of revealing any infraction of the norm, every crime against the rhythms—and therefore implicitly against the order—of society.

On account of their resemblance to the vulva, the marine shell and a number of other species of shells are supposedly preservative against all magic, either of the *jettatura* or of the *mal'-occhio*. Necklaces of shells, or bracelets or amulets ornamented with sea-shells, or even the mere images of them, defend women,

[28] J. W. Jackson, "The Money-Cowry (*Cypraea moneta*, L.) as a sacred object among the American Indians"; *Manchester Memoirs*, Vol. 60, No. 4, 1916, pp. 5 ff.

[29] See Eliade, *Le Chamanisme . . .*, pp. 286.

[30] Jackson, *Shell-Trumpets*, pp. 8, 11, 90; W. H. R. Rivers, *The History of Melanesian Society*, Cambridge, 1914, Vol. I, pp. 69, 98, 186; Vol. II, pp. 459, 535.

[31] Andersson, *Children of the yellow earth*, pp. 306, 312, 307.

children and cattle against misfortunes, illnesses, sterility, etc.[32] The same symbolism—that of assimilation to the very source of the universal Life—strengthens the various efficacies of the shell, either in perpetuating the norms of the cosmic or the social life, promoting a state of well-being and of fecundity, in assuring an easy deliverance to women in labour, or in the spiritual "rebirth" of the neophyte in the course of an initiation ceremony.

THE PART PLAYED BY SHELLS IN FUNERARY BELIEFS

The sexual and gynæcological symbolism of marine shells and oysters implies, we must remember, a spiritual significance also: the "second birth" attained by initiation becomes possible, thanks to the same inexhaustible source from which the life of the cosmos is supplied. Hence also the part played by shells and pearls in funeral customs: one who dies does not separate himself from the cosmic power which has nourished and ruled his life. And in Chinese sepulchres we also find jade impregnated with *yang*—the masculine, solar and "dry" principle—and jade of its own nature resists decomposition. "If there is gold and jade in the nine apertures of the corpse, it will be preserved from putrefaction," writes the alchemist Ko Hung:[33] and Tao Hung Ching (fifth century) gives the following instances: "When, at the opening of an ancient tomb, the corpse looks alive, then there is, inside and outside of the body, a large quantity of gold and of jade. According to the regulations of the Han dynasty, the princes and lords were buried in their clothes adorned with pearls, and with boxes of jade, for the purpose of preserving the body from decay."[34]

[32] Cf. the numerous examples in S. Seligman, *Der böse Blick*, Berlin, 1910, Vol. II, pp. 126 ff., 204 ff.
[33] B. Laufer, *Jade, a Study in Chinese Archæology and Religion*, Field Museum, Chicago, 1912, p. 299, Note.
[34] Laufer, *op. cit.*, p. 299. Cf. also Karlgren, "Some fecundity symbols," pp. 22 ff.; Giseler, "Les Symboles de jade dans le tao-isme" in the *Revue d'Histoire des Religions*, 1932, Vol. 105, pp. 158-181.

Recent researches have confirmed Ko Hung's statement about "the jade which stops up the nine apertures of the corpse", an assertion which had seemed suspect to more than one author.[35]

Jade and shells co-operate in ensuring an excellent destiny in the after-life; while the former preserves the corpse from decomposition, pearls and shells promise a new birth for the deceased. According to Li Ki, the coffin was adorned with "five rows of precious shells" and with "tablets of jade".[36] Besides the *pei* oyster, the Chinese funeral service also made use of the largest and finest of the mussels, *shen*. Mussels and bivalve shells were placed in the bottom of the tomb (Karlgren, *Some fecundity symbols*, p. 41). Cheng Hüan mentions the custom thus: "Before the coffin is to be lowered, one first fills the bottom with *shen* in order to prevent moisture." (*Ibid.*) Pearls were placed in the mouth of the dead person, and "it is stated in the funeral ritual for the Sovereigns (of the Han dynasty) that 'their mouths were filled with rice, and pearls and jade stone were put therein, in accordance with the established ceremonial usages'."[37] Cowries have been found even in the prehistoric settlements of Pu-Chao.[38] And, as we shall see, proto-historic Chinese ceramics also were very often marked by shell symbolism.

Shells play a no less important part in the funeral ceremonies of India. The conch (chank) is sounded and shells are strewn on the road from the dead man's house to the cemetery. In some provinces the mouth of the dead is filled with pearls (Andersson,

[35] C. Hentze, *Les Figurines de la céramique funéraire*, Dresden, 1928, p. V. See also C. Hentze, " Les Jades archaïques en Chine", *Artibus Asiae*, III, 1928-29, pp. 96-110; and "Les Jades Pi et les symboles solaires", *ibid.*, pp. 199-216; Vol. IV, pp. 35-41.

[36] S. Couvreur, *Li Ki*, Vol. II, *Ho Kien Fu*, 2nd edn., 1913, p. 252. Also the same author's *Tso tchuan*, trans. Vol. I, p. 259.

[37] De Groot, *Religious Systems of China*, 1892, I, p. 277.

[38] Andersson, *op. cit.*, p. 323. Cowries are even found in the tombs of the late palæolithic age; see K. Singer, *op. cit.*, p. 50.

p. 299). The custom is found again in Borneo, where a Hindu
influence has probably been grafted on to an autochthonous rite.[39]
In Africa, a layer of shells is spread over the bottom of the tomb.[40]
This was a common custom among a number of ancient American peoples, as we shall see later. Marine and other shells, natural
pearls and artificial pearls have been found in considerable
quantities in prehistoric settlements, most frequently in the
tombs. In the cavern of Laugérie (in the valley of the Vézère in the
Dordogne) dating from the palæolithic, research has brought
to light numerous shells of Mediterranean species, *Cypraea pyrum*
and *C. lurida*. The shells were arranged symmetrically on the
skeleton, by pairs: four on the forehead, one on each hand, two
on each foot, four about the knees and ankles. The cave of
Cavillon contained nearly eight thousand marine shells, most of
them dyed red, and one in ten were perforated.[41] Cro-Magnon
man, for his part, has left us more than three hundred shells of
Littorina littorea, which are perforated. Elsewhere, a female
skeleton covered with shells has been found near the skeleton of a
man wearing ornaments and a crown made of perforated shells.
The man of Combe-Capelle also was adorned with a chain of
perforated shells.[42] This caused Mainage to wonder: "Why was
the skeleton of Laugerie Basse (Dordogne) wearing a necklace of
Mediterranean shells, and the Cro-Magnon skeleton an ornament
built up of ocean shells? Why have the excavations at Grimaldi
(on the Côte d'Azur) yielded shells collected on the shores of the
Atlantic? And how is it that, at Pont-à-Lesse in Belgium, they
have found tertiary shells gathered in the vicinity of Rheims?"[43]

[39] Kunz and Stevenson, *The Book of the Pearl*, p. 310.
[40] Cf. Robert Hertz, *Mélanges de sociologie religieuse et de folklore*, Paris, 1928,
p. 10.
[41] Déchelette, *Manuel d'archéologie préhistorique celtique et gallo-romaine*, 2nd
edn., Paris, 1924, Vol. I, p. 208.
[42] Cf. Osborn, *Men of the Old Stone Age*, pp. 304, 305.
[43] Th. Mainage, *Les Religions de la préhistoire*, I, *L'Age paléolithique*, Paris, 1921,
pp. 96-97.

Nomadism would very probably suffice to explain these facts; but they provide one more proof of the magico-religious importance of shells among the prehistoric peoples.

Shells have also been found in the tombs of pre-dynastic Egypt. The shells of the Red Sea furnished amulets to the Egyptians for a very long time.[44] The Cretan excavations have revealed a singular profusion of shells and shell-work. In a neo-lithic deposit at Phaestos, besides a female image in clay, shells of *petunculus* have been discovered; their religious signification is beyond all doubt.[45] The researches of Sir Arthur Evans have enabled us to define more clearly the magical value and the cult-value of shells. Designs with shell motifs were also abundant, and their persistence has been due less to the decorative value of the motif than to its symbolism.[46] A remarkable discovery, from this point of view, and one which, according to the authoritative opinion of Andersson, proves the transition between the Euro-African cultural cycle and Eastern Asia, was made by Pumpelly at Anu (Andersson, *op. cit.*, p. 298). Andersson in his turn found shells at Yang Chao Thun, and at Sha Ching (in the desert of Chen Fu)—that is, in prehistoric settlements where the funerary urns bear those highly characteristic designs which have been given the names of "death pattern" and "cowrie pattern", and about whose symbolism of "death and resurrection" there is no longer any shadow of doubt (Andersson, *ibid*, pp. 322 ff.). A very ancient Japanese custom is explained by similar beliefs; by anointing one's own body with powdered shell, one is ensuring its re-birth (Kurt Singer, *op. cit.*, p. 51).

The funerary uses of pearls and shells seem to have been of decisive importance among the autochthonous populations of the two Americas. The documentation collected by Jackson is elo-quent enough upon that point.[47] Concerning the Indians of

[44] Sir E. Wallis Budge, *Amulets and Superstitions*, Oxford, 1930, p. 73.

[45] Sir Arthur Evans, *The Palace of Minos*, Vol. I, London, 1921, p. 37.

[46] *Ibid.*, pp. 517 ff., p. 519, figs. 377, 378.

[47] Jackson, "The geographical distribution of the use of Pearls and Pearl-shell",

Florida, Streeter writes that: "As in Cleopatra's time in Egypt, so in Florida, the graves of the kings were decorated with pearls. De Soto's soldiers found, in one of the temples, great wooden coffins in which the dead lay embalmed, and beside them there were small baskets full of pearls. The temple of Tolomecco, however, was the richest in pearls, its high walls and roof were of mother-of-pearl, while strings of pearls and plumes of feathers hung round the walls; over the coffins of the kings hung their shields, and in the centre of the temple stood vases full of costly pearls."[48] Willoughby has already shown the essential part played by pearls in funeral ceremonies, by describing the solemnities of the mummification of the Indian kings of Virginia.[49] Zelia Nuttall has discovered, at the summit of a pyramid in Mexico, a deep layer of shells, in the middle of which were the tombs.[50] And these are but a few of the documents about the American Indians.[51] The presence, in certain regions (Yucatan, for example), of pieces of iron[52] together with pearls and shells, proves that they meant to provide the deceased with all the sources of magical energy at their disposal, for iron, here as in Crete, plays the part that in China devolved upon jade and gold.[53]

---

republished in *Shells as evidence of the migrations of early culture*, pp. 72 ff.; cf pp. 112 ff.

[48] Jackson, *Shells as evidence* . . . pp. 116-117.

[49] C. C. Willoughby, "The Virginian Indians in the seventeenth century", in the *American Anthropologist*, Vol. IX, No. 1, January 1907, (pp. 57-86) pp. 61, 62.

[50] Cf. W. J. Perry, *The Children of the Sun*, p. 66. The Indians who live on the shores of the Gulf of California, whose culture is still extremely primitive, cover their dead with the carapace of a tortoise (*ibid.*, p. 250). The tortoise being by nature an aquatic animal, is closely connected with the waters and with the moon.

[51] Cf. Kunz and Stevenson, *The Book of the Pearl*, pp. 485 ff.

[52] Stephens, *Incidents of Travel in Yucatan*, Vol. II, p. 344, cited by Andree, *Die Metalle bei den Naturvölkers*, Leipzig, 1884, p. 136.

[53] Cf. my *Forgerons et Alchimistes*, Paris, 1956, pp. 20 ff.

In the cave of Mahaxay (Laos), Madeleine Colani has found hatchets, rock crystals and numerous shells of *Cypraea*,[54] and has succeeded, at the same time, in demonstrating the funerary character and magical function of the hatchets.[55] All these objects were deposited in the tomb in order to ensure the best conditions for the deceased in the after life.

Important deposits of oyster shells and marine shells have been discovered in very many prehistoric settlements very far distant from one another. Some *Cypraea moneta*, for example, have been discovered in the famous necropolis of Kuban, north of the Caucasus (fourteenth century B.C.) and other shells in the Scythian tombs of the vicinity of Kiev, which belong to the Ananino civilisation of the western Urals. Analogous deposits have been discovered in Bosnia, in France, in England, in Germany and, above all, on the Baltic coast where the ancients used to look for amber.[56]

The leading part played by pearls in the elaboration of the various mortuary rituals is further shown by the presence of artificial pearls. Nieuwenhuis has studied those—made of stone or porcelain—that were frequently used by the inhabitants of Borneo. The origin of the most ancient of them remains uncertain: the most recent come from Singapore, but were generally manufactured in Europe, at Gablonz (Bohemia), Birmingham or Murano.[57] Madeleine Colani describes the use of these pearls in the solemn agricultural rites, in the sacrifices or funeral ceremonies of Laos, as follows: "The dead are furnished with pearls for the celestial life; these are inserted into the natural orifices of the

[54] Madeleine Colani, "Haches et bijoux. République de l'Équateur, Insulinde, Eurasie" B.E.F.E.O., XXXV, 1935, fasc. 2, pp. 313-362, p. 347.
[55] Cf. also Hanna Rydh, "On Symbolism in mortuary ceramics" in the *Bulletin of the Museum of Far Eastern Antiquities*, No. I, Stockholm, 1929, pp. 71-121, pp. 114 ff.
[56] Andersson, *op. cit.*, pp. 299 ff.; Jackson, *The geographical distribution, passim.*
[57] Nieuwenhuis, "Kunstperlen und ihre kulturelle Bedeutung" in the *Internatl. Archiv. f. Ethnographie*, Bd. 16, pp. 135-153.

corpse. In our own days, the dead are buried with waist-belts, hats and coats adorned with pearls. After the decay of the body, the pearls fall away . . ."[58] The same author has found, buried near the megaliths of the Tran Ninh, quantities of these little gems in glass, sometimes hundreds of them: "These ancient pearls played, in all probability, an important part in the life of the people. . . . Those that we discovered had been buried in the soil to be of service to the dead. They are much simpler than those represented by Mr Nieuwenhuis. Did they have *only* a funerary function? We do not know" (*op. cit.*, p. 199). Near by these archaic pearls there were little bells of bronze. The association of metals with pearls (shells, etc.) is of frequent occurrence elsewhere, and it is maintained in certain regions of the Pacific. Madeleine Colani reminds us that "in Borneo, in our own days, Dyak women wear necklaces with numerous little bells" (*ibid.*, p. 199, fig. 24).

The use of artificial pearls presents a clear case of degradation of the original metaphysical meaning, of its eviction by a secondary, exclusively magical, meaning. The sacred power of pearls came from their marine origin and from a gynæcological symbolism. That all those people who used pearls and shells in their magical and funerary ceremonies were aware of that symbolism is not very likely: even if there were a consciousness of such things it would have been limited to a few members of the society, and such knowledge is not always preserved intact. Whether they borrowed the magical notion of the pearl from peoples of a superior culture with whom they came into contact, or whether their own idea became corrupted under the influence of foreign elements, the fact is that certain peoples introduced into their ceremonies artificial objects whose only recommendation was their resemblance to the "sacred models". This is not the only case. We know that of the cosmological value of lapis lazuli in Mesopotamia: the blue colour of this stone is like that of the starry

[58] Madeleine Colani, "Essai d'Ethnographie comparée" in B.E.F.E.O., Vol XXXVI, 1936, pp. 197-280, pp. 198 ff.

sky, and so participates in its sacred power.[59] An analogous conception is, moreover, found in pre-Columbian America. In
several ancient tombs in an island of Ecuador, twenty-eight
pieces of lapis lazuli have been discovered, cut into cylindrical
form and very beautifully polished. But it has since been ascertained that these pieces of lapis lazuli did not belong to the
inhabitants of the island: in all probability they had been left there
by some visitors from the continent who had come to the island
to perform certain rites or sacred ceremonies.[60]

It is worth noting that in West Africa an exceptional value is
also attributed to artificial blue stones. Wiener has collected a
very rich documentation about this.[61] It is certain that the symbolism and the religious value of these stones find their explanation in the idea of the sacred power in which they participate by
virtue of their celestial colour—an idea frequently unknown, ill-
understood or "debased" by certain elements of these populations,
who have many a time borrowed the object of worship or the
symbol of an advanced culture without adopting its proper
meaning, generally inaccessible to them. One may thus suppose
that the well-known coloured imitation gems which have spread
from Egypt, from Mesopotamia and the Roman Levant right
into the Far East, had, in certain periods, a magical significance
no doubt derived from their natural model or from the geometrical symbolism that they convey.[62]

The sacred virtue of shells extends to *images* of them, as it

---

[59] Ernst Darmstaedter, "Der babylonisch-assyrische Lasurstein", in *Studien für
Geschichte der Chemie, Festgabe Ed. von Lippmann*, Berlin, 1927, pp. 1-8. Cf. my
book, *Cosmologie si alchimie babiloniana*, pp. 51 ff.

[60] George F. Kunz, *The Magic of Jewels and Charms*, Philadelphia-London, 1915,
p. 308.

[61] Leon Wiener, *Africa and the discovery of America*, Philadelphia, 1920-1922,
Vol. II, pp. 237-248; cf. my *Cosmologie si alchimie babiloniana*, pp. 56 ff.

[62] C. G. Seligman and H. C. Beck, "Far Eastern glass: some Western origins",
Bulletin of the Museum of Far Eastern Antiquities, No. 10, Stockholm, 1938, pp.
1-64.

does to the decorative motifs of which the spiral is the essential element. In Kansu numerous funerary urns of the Ma Chang period have been found, ornamented with the "cowrie pattern".[63] Andersson, on the other hand, interprets the figure that predominates on the urn of P'an Shan as a group of four magnificent spirals.[64] A fact worthy of note is that this motif is reserved almost exclusively for funerary urns; it never appears upon pottery for profane uses.[65] The metaphysical and ritual value of the "cowrie-pattern" ("death-pattern") is thus well established. This decorative motif, peculiar to Chinese pottery, plays an active part in the worship of the dead. The image of the shell, or the geometrical elements derived from schematic representations of it, puts the deceased into communication with the cosmic forces that rule fertility, birth and life. For the religious value lies in the *symbolism* of the shell: the *image* is of itself efficacious in the worship of the dead, whether it be present in an actual shell or simply in the form of ornamental motifs of the spiral or the "cowrie pattern". This explains the presence, in Chinese prehistoric settlements, of shells and of funerary urns decorated with the "cowrie pattern".[66]

Nor is the magic function of this motif of funerary decoration attested in China alone. Hanna Rydh has pointed out the resemblances between the "death-pattern" of prehistoric Chinese ceramics and the incised designs upon urns belonging to the Scandinavian megalithic culture.[67] Andersson, on the other hand, notices certain analogies between the urns of Kansu and the

---

[63] Andersson, *Children of the yellow earth*, p. 323; "On symbolism in the prehistoric painted ceramics of China" in the *Bulletin of the Museum of Far Eastern Antiquities*, Vol. I, 1929, pp. 66 ff.

[64] *Children of the yellow earth*, p. 324.

[65] Andersson, "On symbolism in the prehistoric painted ceramics of China", *passim*; Hanna Rydh, *Symbolism in mortuary ceramics*, pp. 81 ff. Cf. Carl Hentze, *Mythes et symboles lunaires*, Antwerp, 1932, p. 118 ff.

[66] Andersson, *Children of the yellow earth*, pp. 323 ff.

[67] *Symbolism in mortuary ceramics*, especially pp. 72 ff.

painted pottery from the south of Russia (Tripolje), analogies
which have also been studied by Professor Bogajevsky. This
spiral motif also turns up again at numerous points in Europe,
America and Asia.[68] We must add, however, that the symbolism
of the spiral is somewhat complex, and that its "origin" is still
uncertain. [69]We may, provisionally at least, take note of the symbolic polyvalency of the spiral, its close relations with the Moon,
with lightning, the waters, fecundity, birth and life beyond
the grave. Moreover, the shell, we may remember, is not used exclusively in the service of the dead. It appears in all the essential
activities of the life of man and of the collectivity: birth, initiation,
marriage, death, agricultural and religious ceremonies, etc.

THE PEARL IN MAGIC AND MEDICINE

The history of the pearl bears further witness to the phenomenon
of the degradation of an initial, metaphysical meaning. What was
at one time a cosmological symbol, an object rich in beneficent
sacred powers, becomes, through the work of time, an element of
ornamentation, appreciated only for its æsthetic qualities and its
economic value. But from the pearl that was an emblem of
absolute *reality* to the pearl of our days that is an "object of value",
the change has taken place by several stages. In medicine, for
instance, both in the East and the West, the pearl has played an
important part. Takkur analyses in detail the medicinal qualities
of the pearl, its use against hæmorrhages and jaundice and as a
cure for demoniac possession and madness.[70] The Hindu author is,
moreover, only continuing a long medical tradition; illustrious
physicians, such as Caraka and Suçruta were even then recom-
mending the use of pearl.[71] Narahari, a Kashmiri physician (of

[68] Madeleine Colani, *Haches et Bijoux*, pp. 351 ff.
[69] Cf. the works of Andersson and Hentze.
[70] Kunz and Stevenson, *op. cit.*, p. 209; Jackson, *Shells as evidence of the migrations
of early culture*, p. 92.
[71] Kunz, *The Magic of Jewels and Charms*, p. 308.

about 1240), writes in his treatise *Rājanigantu* (*varga* XIII) that the pearl cures eye diseases, that it is an effectual antidote in cases of poisoning, that it cures phthisis and, in general, ensures strength and health.[72] It is written in the *Kathāsaritsāgara* that pearl—like the alchemists' elixir—is a defence against "poison, demons, old age and illness". The *Harshacarīta* reminds us that the pearl is born of the tears of the god of the Moon, and that its lunar origin—the moon being a source of eternally curative ambrosia—makes it the antidote to all poisons.[73] In China, medicine made use only of "virgin pearl", not perforated, which was supposed to cure all diseases of the eyes. Identical virtues are ascribed to pearls by Arab medicine.[74]

After the eighth century, the medicinal use of pearls spread also into European medicine, soon giving rise to a great demand for this precious jewel (Kunz and Stevenson, *op. cit.*, p. 18). Albertus Magnus recommends the use of them (*ibid.*, p. 311). Malachias Geiger in his *Margaritologia* (1673) concerns himself exclusively with the medicinal use of pearl, affirming that he had recourse to it, with success, in the treatment of epilepsy, of madness and of melancholy (*ibid.*, p. 312). Francis Bacon lists pearl among the drugs for longevity (*ibid.*, p. 313).

It goes without saying that the use of pearls in the pharmacy of so many diverse civilisations could only come after the importance that they had first acquired in religion and magic. From having been the emblem of the aquatic and generative powers, the pearl became, at a later period, a general tonic, aphrodisiac and at the same time a cure for madness and melancholy, two maladies

---

[72] R. Grabe, *Die Indische Mineralien*, Leipzig, 1882, p. 74.

[73] *Harshacarita*, trans. Cowell and Thomas, pp. 251 ff.

[74] Leclerc, *Traité des simples*, Vol. III, p. 248 (Ibn el-Beithar quotes Ibn Massa and Ishak Ibn Amrān, limiting himself however to medical uses alone); Julius Ruska, *Das Steinbuch der Aristoteles*, Heidelberg, 1912, p. 133; in the popular beliefs of India and Arabia, cf. Penzer, *Ocean of Story*, London, 1924, Vol. I, p. 212, 213 (powdered pearl, remedy for diseases of the eye, etc.).

due to lunar influence[75] and therefore sensitive to any emblem of
Woman, of Water or of Eroticism. Its function in the cure of
diseases of the eyes and as an antidote to poisons is an inheritance
from the mythic relations between pearls and serpents. In many
countries precious stones were believed to be shed from the heads
of serpents, or stored in the throats of dragons.[76] In China, the
dragon's head is supposed always to contain a pearl or some other
precious stone,[77] and more than one work of art depicts a dragon
with a pearl in its mouth.[78] This iconographic motif derives from
a symbolism that is very ancient and rather complex, and would
take us too far away from our theme.[79]

Significant, lastly, is the virtue of promoting longevity that
Francis Bacon ascribes to the pearl. This is indeed one of the
primordial virtues of this precious stone. Its presence on a man's
body, as also that of the shell, connects him with the very sources
of the universal energy, fecundity and fertility. When this sub-
jective image of it no longer corresponded with the new Cosmos
discovered by man, or when the memory of it was corrupted for
other reasons, the formerly sacred object retained its value but that
value itself was expressed upon another level.

On the border-line between magic and medicine, the pearl
plays the ambiguous part of a *talisman*;[80] that which formerly con-

[75] P. Saintyves, *L'Astrologie populaire*, pp. 181 ff.

[76] Cf. my *Patterns in Comparative Religion*, pp. 441, 457 (bibliography). The
essentials are to be found in the study by W. R. Halliday, "Of snakestones" republished in *Folklore Studies*, London, 1924, pp. 132-155.

[77] Cf., for example, De Groot, *Les Fêtes annuellement célébrées à Emouï*, Vol. II,
pp. 369, 385.

[78] Cf. Josef Zykan, "Drache und Perle" in *Artibus Asiae*, VI, 1-2, 1936, pp. 5-16,
p. 9, fig. I, etc.

[79] Cf. Alfred Salmony, "The magic ball and the golden fruit in ancient Chinese
art", in *Art and thought; Homage to Coomaraswamy*, London, 1947, pp. 105-109;
see also my *Patterns in Comparative Religion*, pp. 288 ff.

[80] S. Seligman, *Der böse Blick*, II, pp. 126, 209; id., *Die Magische Heil- und
Schutzmittel*, p. 199.

ferred fertility and assured one of an ideal destiny *post mortem* became, little by little, a steady source of prosperity.[81] In India, this conception lingered on until fairly lately. "Pearls should always be worn by those who desire prosperity," said Buddha-batta.[82] The proof that pearls entered into medicine because of the part that they had previously played in magic and in erotic and funerary symbolism, is that in some countries shells have a medicinal virtue. In China, they are as familiar to the doctor as they are precious to the magician.[83] So they are among certain American tribes.[84]

Apart from their recognised value in magic and medicine, shells have frequently been used as money. The evidence for this furnished by Jackson and other authors, is sufficient proof of it.[85] Karlgren, who has demonstrated the monetary use of shells in China, believes that the custom of wearing a coin on the forehead is an inheritance from the time when the shell was still commonly worn as an amulet.[86] The sacred-symbolical value of the marine shell and of the pearl became gradually secularised. But the *preciousness* of the object has by no means suffered in this displacement of values. The *power* remains concentrated in it all the time; it is force and substance; it remains steadily identified with the "reality" of life and fertility.

[81] The pearl as a guarantee against epidemics, giving courage to its wearer, etc., see M. Gaster, "The Hebrew version of the Secretum Secretorum" republished in *Studies and Texts*, Vol. II, London, 1925-1928, p. 812.

[82] Louis Finot, *Les Lapidaires indiens*, p. 16; Kunz, *op. cit.*, p. 316.

[83] Karlgren, *op. cit.*, p. 36.

[84] Jackson, *The Money Cowry (Cypraea moneta, L.) as a sacred object among the American Indians*, pp. 3 ff.

[85] Cf. "The Use of Cowry-shells for the purposes of currency, amulets and charms" in *Manchester Memoirs*, 1916, No. 13; *Shells* pp. 123-194; Leo Wiener, *Africa and the discovery of America*, pp. 203 ff.; Helmut Petri, "Die Geldformen der Südsee" in *Anthropos*, 31, 1936, pp. 187-212, 509-554; pp. 193 ff., 509 ff. (cowries as money), 208 ff. (pearls as money).

[86] Karlgren, *op. cit.*, p. 34.

THE MYTH OF THE PEARL

Archetypal images keep their metaphysical valencies intact in spite of later "concrete" re-valorisations: the commercial value of the pearl in no way abolishes its religious symbolism; this is continually being rediscovered, reintegrated and enriched. Let us recall, indeed, the considerable part played by the pearl in Iranian speculation, in Christianity and in Gnosticism. A tradition of Eastern origin explains the birth of the pearl as the child of lightning penetrating into a mussel;[87] the pearl thus being the result of union between Fire and Water. St Ephrem makes use of this ancient myth to illustrate the Immaculate Conception as well as the spiritual birth of the Christ in the baptism of Fire.[88]

On the other hand, Stig Wikander has shown that the pearl was the supreme Iranian symbol of the Saviour.[89] The identification of the Pearl with the "Saviour saved" rendered a double meaning possible: the Pearl could represent the Christ as well as the human soul. Origen renews the identification of the Christ with the Pearl, and is followed by numerous authors (Edsman, *op. cit.*, pp. 192 ff.). In a text of the pseudo-Macarius, the pearl symbolises on the one hand the Christ as King, and on the other the descendant of the King, the Christian: "The Pearl, great, precious and royal, belonging to the royal diadem, is appropriate only to the king. The king alone may wear this pearl. No one else is allowed to wear a pearl like it. Thus, a man who is not born

[87] Cf. Pauly-Wissova, s.v. *Margaritai*, col. 1692.

[88] H. Usener, "Die Perle. Aus der Geschichte eines Bildes" in the *Theologische Abhandlungen C. von Weizsäcker . . . gewidmet*, Freiburg i. Breisgau, 1892, pp. 201-213; Carl-Martin Edsman, *Le Baptême de feu*, Leipzig-Uppsala, 1940, pp. 190 ff.

[89] Review of Edsman's book in the *Svensk Teologisk Kvartalskrift*, Vol. 17, 1945, pp. 228-233: cf. Geo. Widengren, *Mesopotamian elements in Manicheism*, Uppsala, 1946, p. 119; *id.*, "Der Iranische Hintergrund der Gnosis" in the *Zeitschrift für Religions- und Geistesgeschichte*, IV, 1952 (pp. 97-114), p. 113.

of the royal and divine spirit, and is not one of the sons of God—
of whom it is written that: 'as many as received him, to them gave
he power to become the sons of God'—cannot wear the precious,
heavenly pearl, image of the ineffable light which is the Saviour.
For he has not become a son of the king. Those who wear and
possess the pearl will live and reign with the Christ for all eternity."[90]

In the famous Gnostic scripture, the *Acts of Thomas*, the quest
of the pearl symbolises the spiritual drama of the fall of man and
his salvation; a Prince from the Orient arrives in Egypt in search
of the Pearl, which is guarded by monstrous serpents. To obtain
it, the Prince has to pass through a number of initiatory trials;
nor can he succeed without the aid of his father, the King of
Kings—a Gnostic image for the heavenly Father.[91] The symbolism
in this text is rather complicated: the Pearl represents, on the one
hand, the fallen soul of man in the world of darkness, and, on the
other, the "Saviour saved" himself. The identification of man
with the pearl is to be found in a number of Manichæan and
Mandæan texts. The Living spirit "snatches the First Man out of
the struggle like a pearl drawn out of the sea".[92] St Ephrem compares the mystery of baptism to a pearl which can never be
acquired again: "the diver, too, takes the pearl out of the sea.
Dive! [be baptised], take from the water the purity hidden in it,
the pearl out of which comes the crown of divinity!" (Quoted by
Edsman, p. 197.)

Upon another occasion, discussing the subject of ascetics and
monks, St Ephrem compares their asceticism to "a second
baptism": just as the pearl-diver has to plunge naked into the
ocean and make his way among the monsters of the deep, so do

[90] *Homélie* XXIII, 1; text quoted and translated by Edsman, *op. cit.*, pp. 192-193.
[91] A. Hilgenfeld, "Der Königssohn und die Perle", *Zeitschrift für wissenschaft-
liche Theologie*, Vol. 47, 1904, pp. 219-249; R. Reitzenstein, *Das iranische
Erlösungsmysterium*, Bonn, 1921, pp. 72 ff. (an essential work); Edsman, *op. cit.*,
p. 193, Note 4; Widengren, *Der iranische Hintergrund der Gnosis*, pp. 105 ff.
[92] *Kephalaia*, p. 85, cited by Edsman, p. 195.

the ascetics go naked "among the men of this world" (Edsman, p. 198). Besides the symbolism of nudity, we can discern in this text an allusion to the marine monsters who lie in wait for the catechumen during his baptismal immersion (see the following chapter, pp. 154 ff.). The gnosis is "hidden" and hard to attain; the path of salvation is strewn with obstacles. The pearl symbolises all this and yet more besides; its appearance in this phenomenal world is miraculous, its presence among fallen beings is paradoxical. The pearl signifies the mystery of the transcendent revealed to the senses, the manifestation of God in the Cosmos. Thanks to Gnosticism and to Christian theology, this ancient symbol of Reality and of the Life-without-Death acquired new valencies; the immortal soul, the "Saviour saved", the Christ-King. Let us underline once more the *continuity* of the various meanings of the pearl, from the most archaic and elementary to the most complex symbolisms elaborated by gnostic and orthodox speculation.

V

Symbolism and History

Among the few groups of symbols we have just presented that belong to the aquatic realm, this last is by far the most vast and complex. We have tried to elucidate its structure in a previous work, to which we refer the reader—*Patterns in Comparative Religion*, pp. 188 ff.—where he will find the essential data from a dossier on the aquatic hierophanies, and with these an analysis evaluating their symbolism. Here we will limit ourselves to a few of its most important features.

The Waters symbolise the entire universe of the virtual; they are the *fons et origo*, the reservoir of all the potentialities of existence; they *precede* every form and *sustain* every creation. The exemplary image of the whole creation is the Island that suddenly "manifests" itself amidst the waves. Conversely, immersion in the waters symbolises a regression into the pre-formal, reintegration into the undifferentiated mode of pre-existence. Emergence repeats the cosmogonic act of formal manifestation; while immersion is equivalent to a dissolution of forms. That is why the symbolism of the Waters includes Death as well as Re-Birth. Contact with water always goes with a regeneration, on the one hand because dissolution is followed by a "new birth", and on the other hand because immersion fertilises and multiplies the potentialities of life. To the aquatic cosmogony correspond—at the anthropological level—the hylogenies, the beliefs according to which mankind is born of the Waters. To the deluge, or to the periodical submergence of continents (myths of the "Atlantis" type), there corresponds, at the human level, the "second death" of the soul (the "humidity" and *leimon* of Hell, etc.) or the initiatory death by baptism. But, upon the cosmological no less than upon the anthropomorphic plane, immersion in the Waters signifies, not a definitive extinction but a temporary re-entry into the indistinct, followed by a new creation, a new life or a new man, according to whether the nature of the event in question is cosmic, biological or soteriological. From the point of view of structure, the "deluge" is comparable to a "baptism", and the funerary libation to the lustrations of the newly-born, or to the ritual bathings in the Spring that procure health and fertility.

In whatever religious context we find them, the Waters invariably preserve their function: they dissolve or abolish the forms of things, "wash away sins", are at once purifying and regenerative. It is their lot both to precede the Creation and to re-absorb it, incapable as they are of surpassing their own modality—that is, of manifesting themselves in *forms*. The Waters cannot get beyond the state of the virtual, of seeds and of what is latent. Everything that has form manifests itself above the Waters, by detaching itself from them. On the other hand, as soon as it is separated from the waters and has ceased to be potential (virtual), every form comes under the laws of Time and of Life; it acquires limitations, participates in the universal becoming, is subject to history, decays away and is finally emptied of substance unless it be regenerated by periodic immersions in the Waters, repetitions of the "deluge" with its cosmogonic corollary. The purpose of the ritual lustrations and purifications is to gain a flash of realisation of the non-temporal moment (*in illo tempore*) in which the creation took place; they are symbolical repetitions of the birth of worlds or of the "new man".

One point that is essential here, is that the sacredness of the Waters and the structure of the aquatic cosmologies and apocalypses could never have been wholly revealed except through the aquatic symbolism, which is the only "system" capable of integrating all the particular revelations of the innumerable hierophanies (see my *Patterns in Comparative Religion*, p. 449). This is, moreover, the law for all symbolism: it is the *entire* symbolism which gives value to (and corrects!) the various meanings of the hierophanies. The "Waters of Death", for example, reveal their profound meaning only to the degree that one knows the structure of the aquatic symbolism. This peculiarity of symbolism is not without consequences for the "experiencing" or the "history" of any one symbol.

In our retracing of the main outlines of the aquatic symbology, we kept one precise point in view—namely, the new religious values conferred upon Water by Christianity. The Fathers of the Church did not fail to exploit some of the pre-Christian and universal values of the Water-symbolism, retaining freedom to enrich it with new meanings in relation to the Christian historical drama. We have referred elsewhere (in *Patterns in Comparative Religion*, pp. 196 ff.) to two patristic texts, one dealing with the soteriological values of water and the other with the baptismal symbolism of death and rebirth. For Tertullian (*De Baptismo*, III-V), water was the first "seat of the divine Spirit, who then preferred it to all the other elements. . . . It was water that was first commanded to produce living creatures . . . it was water which, first of all, produced that which has life, so that we should not be astonished when, one day, it would bring forth life in baptism. In the formation of man himself, God made use of water to consummate his work . . . all natural water thus acquired, by ancient prerogatives with which it was honoured at its origin, the virtue of sanctification in the sacrament, provided that God be invoked to that effect. As soon as the words are pronounced, the Holy Spirit, coming down from Heaven, hovers over the waters, which it sanctifies by its fecundity: the waters thus sanctified are in their turn impregnated with sanctifying virtue. . . . That which formerly healed the body, today cures the soul; that which procured health in time procures salvation in eternity. . . ."

The "old man" dies by immersion in the water, and gives birth to a new regenerated being. This symbolism is admirably expressed by John Chrysostom (*Homil. in Joh.*, XXV, 2) who, speaking of the symbolic multivalency of baptism, writes: "It represents death and entombment, life and resurrection. . . . When we plunge our head into water, as into a sepulchre, the old man is immersed, altogether buried: when we come out of the water the new man simultaneously appears."

As we see, the interpretations given by Tertullian and John Chrysostom harmonise perfectly with the structure of aquatic symbolism. However, certain new elements that enter into this Christian revaluation of Water are bound up with a "history"—namely, Sacred History. The recent works of P. Lundberg, Jean Daniélou and Louis Beirnaert have amply demonstrated the extent to which baptismal symbolism is saturated with Biblical allusions.[1] First of all, there is the valorisation of baptism as a descent into the abyss of the Waters to fight a duel with the sea monster. There is a pattern for this—the descent of the Christ into Jordan, which was at the same time a descent into the Waters of Death. Cyril of Jerusalem in fact presents the descent into the baptismal font, a descent into the water of death inhabited by the dragon of the sea, as an image of the Christ going down into the Jordan during his baptism, in order to break the power of the dragon who is hidden there: "The dragon Behemoth, according to Job," writes Cyril, "was in the waters and received the Jordan in its maw. But, as the heads of the dragon had to be broken, Jesus, after descending into the waters, bound him fast, so that we might acquire the power of walking over scorpions and ser-

---

[1] P. Lundberg, *La Typologie baptismale dans l'ancienne Église*, Uppsala-Leipzig, 1942; Jean Daniélou, S. J., *Sacramentum Futuri. Études sur les origines de la typologie biblique*, Paris, 1950, pp. 13-20, 55-85 *et passim*; *id.*, *Bible et Liturgie*, Paris, 1951, pp. 29-173; Louis Beirnaert, S.J., "La dimension mythique dans le sacramentalisme chrétien", in the *Eranos-Jahrbuch*, 1949, Vol. XVII, Zürich, 1950, pp. 255-286. The fine books of Lundberg and Daniélou also contain copious bibliographical information.

pents . . ."[2] Still advising the catechumen, Cyril proceeds: "The dragon lurks by the side of the road, watching those who pass by; take care that he bite thee not! Thou goest to the Father of spirits, but must needs pass by this dragon" (quoted in Beirnaert, p. 272). As we shall see, this descent and struggle with the marine monster constitute an initiatory ordeal that is attested in other religions also.

After this comes the evaluation of baptism as an *antitypos* of the Flood. Christ, the new Noah, rising victorious from the Waters, has become the head of a new race (Justin, cited by Daniélou, *Sacramentum futuri*, p. 74). Moreover, the Deluge prefigures the descent into the depths of the sea, as well as baptism. According to Irenæus, it is the image of salvation by the Christ and of the judgment upon sinners (Daniélou, *loc. cit.*, p. 72). "The Deluge, then, was an image that baptism came to realise . . . Even as Noah had faced the sea of death in which sinful humanity had been annihilated, and had come out of it, so has the newly baptised descended into the baptismal font to confront the dragon of the sea in a supreme combat and to emerge victorious . . ." (*ibid.*, p. 65).

But—still in reference to the baptismal rite—the Christ is also compared with Adam. The parallel between Adam and Christ had already played a considerable part in the theology of St Paul. "Through baptism," affirms Tertullian, "man regains resemblance to God" (*De Baptismo*, V). For St Cyril, "baptism is not only the cleansing from sin and the grace of adoption, but also an antitype of the passion of Christ" (quoted in Daniélou, *Bible et Liturgie*, p. 61). The baptismal nakedness, too, conveys a meaning that is at once ritual and metaphysical: it is the abandonment of the "old vesture of corruption and sin which the baptised person has put off to follow Christ, and in which Adam had been clothed since the Fall" (Daniélou, *op. cit.*, p. 55), but it is also the return to original innocence, to the condition of Adam before the Fall: "O

[2] J. Daniélou, *Bible et Liturgie*, pp. 58-59; see also his *Sacramentum futuri*, pp. 58 ff.; Lundberg, *op. cit.*, pp. 148 ff.

how wonderful it is!" writes Cyril. "You were naked before the eyes of all, without feeling ashamed of it. Verily, that is because you bear within you the image of the first Adam who was naked in Paradise without feeling ashamed" (cited by Daniélou, *op. cit.*, p. 56).

The baptismal symbolism is even richer yet in Biblical references, and above all in paradisiac reminiscences; but these few texts will suffice for our purpose, which is not so much to describe this symbolism as to account for the innovations brought into it by Christianity. The Fathers of the primitive Church envisaged this symbolism almost entirely as a typology; they were primarily concerned to discover correspondences between the two Testaments.[3] Modern authors are inclined to follow their example: instead of replacing Christian symbolism in the framework of

[3] Let us recall the meaning and the basis of this typology. "Its point of departure is found in the Old Testament itself. The Prophets, indeed, announced to the people of Israel, during their captivity, that in the future God would do for them works similar to, and yet greater than, those that he had accomplished in the past. Thus, there was to be a new Deluge which would annihilate the sinful world, from which, however, a remnant would be preserved to inaugurate a new humanity; there was to be another Exodus in which God, by his power, would set mankind free from bondage to idols; there would be a new Paradise into which God was to lead his liberated people. This constitutes a primary typology that we might call eschatological, for these events to come are, to the prophets, those of the last times. The New Testament, then, did not invent this typology, but only showed that it was all accomplished in the person of Jesus of Nazareth. Indeed, with Jesus, the events of the end, of 'the fullness of time', are consummated: he is the New Adam, and with him the time of the future Paradise has arrived. Already realised in him is the destruction of the sinful world that the Deluge prefigures. In him is accomplished the true Exodus, which liberates the people of God from the tyranny of the Devil. The apostolic preaching employed typology as an argumentative method to establish the truth of its message, by showing that the Christ continued and surpassed the Old Testament: 'These things happened as a figure (*typikos*) and were written for our instruction' (*I Corinthians*, X, 11): That is what St Paul calls the *consolatio Scripturarum*." (J. Daniélou, *Bible et Liturgie*, pp. 9-10.)

symbolism "in general", as it is universally attested by the religions of the non-Christian world, they persist in relating it solely to the Old Testament. According to these authors it is not the general and immediate meaning of the symbol, but its Biblical valorisation that Christian symbolism ought to convey.

This attitude is perfectly understandable. The trend of Biblical and typological studies during the last quarter of a century shows a reaction against the tendency to explain Christianity by means of the mysteries and of syncretic Gnosticism, and also a reaction against the "confusionism" of certain comparativist schools. Christian liturgy and symbology are connected directly with Judaism. Christianity is a historic religion, deeply rooted in another historic religion, that of the Jews. Consequently, in order to explain or better to understand certain sacraments or symbols, one has only to look for their "prefigurations" in the Old Testament. In the historicist perspective of Christianity that is only natural: revelation has had a *history*; the primitive revelation, operative in the dawn of time, still survives among the nations, but it is half-forgotten, mutilated, corrupted; it is to be approached only through the history of Israel; the revelation is fully conserved only in the sacred books of the Old Testament. As we shall see later, Judæo-Christianity tries not to lose contact with sacred history which, unlike the "history" of all other nations, is the only *real* history and the only one with a meaning, for it is God himself who makes it.

Careful above all to attach themselves to a *history* which is at the same time a *revelation*, careful not to be confused with the "initiates" of the various religions and mysteries, the multiple gnosticisms that were swarming around the dying world of antiquity, the Fathers of the Church were obliged to take up the polemical position that they did. To reject all "paganism" was indispensable for the triumph of the message of the Christ. We may wonder whether this polemical attitude is still as strictly necessary in our own day. I am not speaking theologically, for

which I have neither the responsibility nor the competence. But
to anyone who does not feel himself accountable for the faith of
his fellow men, it seems evident that the Judæo-Christian symbolism of baptism in no way contradicts the universally diffused
symbolism of water. Everything reappears in it: Noah and the
Flood have their counterparts in numerous traditions where some
cataclysm puts an end to a whole "humanity" (or "society") with
the exception of a single man who becomes the mythical Ancestor
of a new humanity. The "Waters of Death" are the *leitmotif* of various palæo-oriental, Asiatic and Oceanian mythologies. The
"Water" is pre-eminently "killing": it dissolves, it abolishes all
forms. That is just why it is rich in creative "seeds". Nor is the
symbolism of the baptismal nakedness a privileged peculiarity of
the Judæo-Christian tradition. Ritual nudity is expressive of
integrity and plenitude; "Paradise" implies the absence of
"clothing"—that is, of "wear and tear" (an archetypal image of
Time). As for the nostalgia for Paradise, it is universal, although
its manifestations vary almost indefinitely.[4] All ritual nakedness
implies an a-temporal paradigm, a paradisiac image.

The monsters of the abyss reappear in a number of traditions:
the Heroes, the Initiates, go down into the depths of the abyss to
confront marine monsters; this is a typical ordeal of initiation.
Variants indeed abound: sometimes a dragon mounts guard over
a "treasure"—a sensible image of the sacred, of absolute reality.
The ritual (that is, initiatory) victory over the monstrous guardian
is equivalent to the conquest of immortality.[5] For the Christian,
baptism is a sacrament because it was instituted by the Christ. But,
none the less for that, it repeats the initiatory ritual of the ordeal
(i.e., the struggle against the monster), of death and of the symbolic resurrection (the birth of the new man). I am not saying that
Judaism or Christianity have "borrowed" such myths or such
symbols from the religions of neighbouring peoples—that was
not necessary. Judaism had inherited a long religious history and

[4] Cf. also *Patterns in Comparative Religion*, pp. 382 ff.
[5] Cf. *Patterns in Comparative Religion*, pp. 207 ff., 290 ff.

prehistory in which all these things existed already. It was not even necessary that this or that symbol should have been kept "awake" in its integrity by Judaism; it was enough that a group of images survived, though obscurely, from pre-Mosaic times: such images were capable of conveying, at no matter what moment, a powerful religious actuality.

Certain Fathers of the Church have examined the interesting correspondence between the archetypal images evoked by Christianity and the Images which are the common property of mankind. One of their most constant concerns is, precisely, to make manifest to unbelievers the correspondence between those great symbols which the soul finds immediately expressive and persuasive, and the dogmas of the new religion. Speaking to those who deny the resurrection of the dead, Theophilus of Antioch appeals to the signs ($\tau\varepsilon\chi\mu\tilde{\eta}\rho\iota\alpha$) that God puts within their reach in those great phenomena of Nature, the beginning and end of the seasons, and of day and night. He goes so far as to say: "Is there not a resurrection for the seeds and the fruits?" For Clement of Rome, "day and night show us the resurrection: the night descends, the day breaks; the day departs and night arrives" (Beirnaert, *op. cit.*, p. 275). For the Christian apologists, the Images were charged with signs and messages; they *showed forth* the sacred by means of the cosmic rhythms. The revelation conveyed by the Faith did not dispel the "primary" meanings of the Images; it simply added a new value to them. For the believer, it is true, this new meaning eclipsed all others: it *alone* valorised the Image, transfiguring it into Revelation. It was the Resurrection of the Christ that mattered, and not the "signs" that one could read in Nature: in the majority of cases, one did not understand the "signs" until after having found the Faith in the depths of one's soul. But the mystery of faith is a matter for Christian experience, for theology and religious psychology and surpasses our present research. In the perspective I have chosen, one thing alone is important: that *every new valorisation has always been conditioned by the actual structure of the Image*, so much so that we can say of an Image that it is *awaiting* the fulfilment of its meaning.

Proceeding to an analysis of the baptismal Images, the Rev. Fr. Beirnaert recognises "a relation between the dogmatic statements, the symbology of the Christian religion and the archetypes activated by the natural symbols. How, moreover, could the candidates for baptism understand the symbolic images put before them if these did not respond to their obscure expectations?" (*op. cit.*, p. 276). The author is not surprised that "many Catholics should have rediscovered the way of faith through such experiences" (*ibid.*). Of course, continues Fr. Beirnaert, the experience of the archetypes does not encroach upon the experience of the faith: "People may meet together in a common recognition of the relations of religious symbols to the psyche, and still class themselves as believers or as unbelievers. The faith, then, is something other than this recognition [. . .] The act of faith brings about a division of the world of archetypal representations. Henceforth the serpent, the darkness, Satan, designate that which one renounces. One recognises, as the only representations capable of mediating salvation, those that are put forward as such by the historic community" (*ibid.* p. 277).

ARCHETYPAL IMAGES AND CHRISTIAN SYMBOLISM

Nevertheless, Fr. Beirnaert recognises that, even if the imagery and symbolism of the Christian sacraments do not direct the believer's mind "primarily to the myths and immanent archetypes, but to the intervention of the divine Power in history, this new meaning must not lead us to deny the permanence of the ancient meaning. By its renewal of the great figures and symbolisations of natural religion, Christianity has also renewed their vitality and their power in the depths of the psyche. The mythic and archetypal dimension remains none the less real for being henceforth subordinate to another. The Christian may well be a man who has ceased to look for his spiritual salvation in myths and in experience of the immanent archetypes alone; he has not, for all that, abandoned all that the myths and symbolisms mean and do to the psychic man, to the microcosm [. . .] The adoption, by Christ and the Church, of the great images of the sun, the moon, of wood, water, the sea and so forth, amounts to an evangelisation of the effective powers that they denote. The Incarnation must not be reduced to the taking-on of the flesh alone. God has intervened even in the collective unconscious, that it may be saved and fulfilled. The Christ descended into hell. How, then, can this salvation reach into our unconsciousness without speaking its language and making use of its categories?" (Beirnaert, *op. cit.*, pp. 284-285.)

This text provides some important elucidations of the relations between "immanent" symbols and faith. As we have seen, the problem of faith lies outside our present deliberations. One aspect of it, however, is of interest to us: the Christian faith is dependent on a *historic* revelation: it is the manifestation of God in Time which, in the eyes of a Christian, ensures the validity of the Images and the symbols. We have seen that the "immanent" and universal symbology of water was not abolished nor dismembered in consequence of the local and historical Judæo-Christian inter-pretations of baptismal symbolism. To put it in a rather simplified way: history does not radically modify the structure of an "immanent" symbolism. History continually adds new meanings to it, but these do not destroy the structure of the symbol. We shall see, later on, what consequences follow from this for the philosophy of history and the morphology of culture: but for the moment, let us look at a few more examples.

We have already discussed (pp. 44 ff.) the symbolism of the Tree of the World. Christianity has utilised, interpreted and amplified this symbol. The Cross, made of the wood of the tree of good and evil, appears in the place of this Cosmic Tree; the Christ himself is described as a Tree (by Origen). A homily of the pseudo-Chrysostom speaks of the Cross as a tree which "rises from the earth to the heavens. A plant immortal, it stands at the centre of heaven and of earth; strong pillar of the universe, bond of all things, support of all the inhabited earth; cosmic inter-lacement, comprising in itself the whole medley of human nature . . ." "And the Byzantine liturgy sings even now, on the day of the exaltation of the Holy Cross, of 'the tree of life planted on Calvary, the tree on which the King of ages wrought our salvation', the tree which 'springing from the depths of the earth, has risen to the centre of the earth' and 'sanctifies the Universe unto its limits'."[6] The Image of the Cosmic Tree is preserved in astonishing purity. Its prototype is, very probably, to be sought in that Wisdom which, according to Proverbs III, 18, "is a tree of life to those who lay hold of her." Fr. de Lubac writes of this Wisdom (*op. cit.*, p. 71) that "for Jews, this will be the Law; for Christians, it will be the Son of God". Another probable proto-type is the tree that Nebuchadnezzar saw in a dream (*Daniel*, IV, 7-15): " I saw, and behold, a tree in the midst of the earth; and its height was great," etc.

Fr. de Lubac admits that, like the symbol of the Cosmic Tree of Indian tradition, the image of the Cross as the Tree of the World is a continuation into Christianity of "an old, universal myth" (*op. cit.*, p. 75). But he is careful to draw attention to the innovations made by Christianity. We find, for instance, in the sequel to the homily of the pseudo-Chrysostom, that the Uni-verse is the Church: " she is the new macrocosm, of which the Christian soul is the analogue in miniature" (*ibid.*, p. 77). And how many other striking differences there are between the Buddha and the Christ, between the pillar of Sanchi and the Cross (*ibid.*, pp. 77 ff.). For all his conviction that the utilisation of such an image by both Buddhism and Christianity "is after all only a matter of language" (p. 76), the eminent theologian seems to exaggerate the importance of historical specificities: "The whole

[6] Henri de Lubac, *Aspects du Bouddhisme*, Paris, 1951, pp. 57, 66-77. Upon this problem, see R. Bauerreiss, *Arbor Vitae. "Lebensbaum" und seine Verwendung in Liturgie, Kunst und Brauchtum des Abendlandes*, Munich, 1938, Abhandlungen der Bayerischen Benediktiner-Akademie, III.

question is, in each case, that of finding out the kind and the degree of originality in the 'particular version' " (*ibid.*, p. 169, Note 101).

Is that really the whole question? Are we in fact condemned to be content with exhaustive analyses of "particular versions" which, when all is said and done, represent local histories? Have we no means of approach to the Image, the symbol, the archetype, in their own structures; in that "wholeness" which embraces all their "histories", without, however, confusing them? There are numerous patristic and liturgical texts which compare the Cross to a ladder, a column or a mountain (de Lubac, pp. 64-68). And these, we may remember, are universally attested formulas for the "Centre of the World". It is in this aspect, as a symbol of the Centre of the World, that the Cross has been likened to the Cosmic Tree; which is a proof that the Image of the Centre *imposed itself naturally* upon the Christian mind. It is by the Cross (= the Centre) that communication with Heaven is opened and that, by the same token, the entire Universe is "saved" (see above, p. 43). *But the notion of "salvation" does no more than repeat and complete the notions of perpetual renovation and cosmic regeneration, of universal fecundity and of sanctity, of absolute reality and, in the final reckoning, of immortality*—all of which co-exist in the symbolism of the Tree of the World.[7]

Let it be well understood that I am not denying the importance of history, or in the case of Judæo-Christianity of faith, for the estimation of the true value of this or that symbol *as it was understood and lived in a specific culture*: we shall indeed underline this later. But it is not by "placing" a symbol in its own history that we can resolve the essential problem—namely, to know what is revealed to us, not by any "particular version" of a symbol but by the *whole* of a symbolism. We have already seen how the various meanings of a symbol are linked together, interconnected in a system, as it were. The contradictions one can discover between the various particular versions are in most cases

[7] Cf. my *Patterns in Comparative Religion*, pp. 266 ff.

only apparent; they are resolved as soon as we consider the symbolism as a whole and discern its structure. Each new valorisation of an archetypal Image crowns and consummates the earlier ones: the "salvation" revealed by the Cross does not annul the pre-Christian values of the Tree of the World, that pre-eminent symbol of the total *renovatio*; on the contrary, the Cross comes to complete all its earlier valencies and meanings.[8] Let us observe, once more, that this new valorisation, brought about by the identification of the Cosmic Tree with the Cross, took place *in* history and through a historical event—the Passion of Christ. As we shall see, the great originality of Judæo-Christianity was the transfiguration of History into theophany.

Here is another example. We know that the shaman goes down into hell to seek and to bring back his patient's soul, which has been snatched away by demons.[9] Orpheus, similarly, descends into

[8] This symbolism is confirmed by the fact that, in the decorations of baptisteries, the Tree of Life is often accompanied by the stag—another archaic image of cyclic renewal (cf. H. C. Puech, "Le Cerf et le Serpent" in the *Cahiers archéologiques*, IV, 1949, pp. 17-60, especially pp. 29 ff). But, in prehistoric China, in the Altaï and in certain cultures of Central and of North America (above all the Maya and the Pueblo) the stag is one of the symbols of continual creation and renewal, simply because of the periodic renewal of its antlers: cf. C. Hentze, "Comment il faut lire l'iconographie d'un vase en bronze chinois de la période Chang", *Conferenze* I.S.M.E.O., Vol. I, Rome, 1951 (pp. 1-60) pp. 24 ff.; *id.*, *Bronzegerät, Kultbauten, Religion im ältesten China der Shang-Zeit*, Antwerp, 1951, pp. 210 ff. In the Greek traditions the stag renewed its life by eating serpents and then, without delay, drinking from the waters of a spring: the antlers then fell away, and the stag was rejuvenated for fifty, or five hundred years (for references, see Puech, *op. cit.*, p. 29). The enmity between the stag and the serpent is of a cosmological order: the stag is related to fire and to the dawn (China, Altaï, America, etc.); the serpent is one of the images of Night and of the larval, underground life. But the serpent also is a symbol of periodical renovation, although upon another plane. In fact, the opposition between the stag (or the eagle) and the serpent is rather of the nature of a "pair of opposites" that have to be reintegrated.

[9] For all this, see my book, *Le Chamanisme et les techniques de l'extase*, Paris, 1951.

hell to bring back his wife Eurydice who has just died. There are analogous myths elsewhere; in Polynesia, in North America, and in Central Asia (here, the myth is constitutive of an oral literature of shamanic structure); a hero is said to descend into hell to recover the soul of his dead wife. In the Polynesian and Central Asian myths he succeeds in this: in the North American myths he fails, in the same way as Orpheus. We will not hasten to draw any conclusion at all from this, but let us register one detail: Orpheus is the bard, the charmer of wild beasts, physician, poet and civilising hero: in short, he combines exactly those functions that fall to the lot of the shaman in "primitive" societies. The shaman is more than the healer and the specialist in techniques of ecstasy: he is also the friend and master of wild animals: he imitates their cries; he transforms himself into an animal; he is, moreover, bard, poet and civiliser. Let us remember, lastly, that Jesus also descends into Hell to save Adam, to restore the integrity of man who is fallen through sin—and that one of the consequences of the fall of man was the loss of his dominion over the animals.

Have we then the right to regard Orpheus as a "shaman" or to compare the descent of Christ into Hell with the descents of the shamans in a state of trance? Everything is against it: in the various cultures and religions—Siberian or North American, Greek or Judæo-Christian—these descents are valued in very different ways. It is needless to enlarge upon the differences, they are so obvious. But one element remains immutable, and must not be lost sight of; that is, the theme of the descent into Hell *for the sake of the salvation of a soul*, whether it be the soul of someone who is ill (shamanism *stricto sensu*), or of the spouse (Greek, North American, Polynesian or Central Asiatic myths) or of the whole of humanity (as with the Christ), concerns us little at the moment. In this case the descent is no longer only initiatory, or undertaken for a personal advantage; it has a "redemptive" aim: one "dies" and "resurrects", not now to complete an initiation already acquired, but to save a soul. A new element characterises the archetype of initiation; the symbolic death is no longer undergone solely for one's own spiritual perfection (more exactly, for the conquest of immortality), but for the salvation of *others*. I am in no way trying to demonstrate, either in the primitive shaman or in the North American or Polynesian Orpheus, a prefiguration of the Christ. I am only pointing out that the archetype of initiation also includes this valency of "death" (= descent into Hell) for the sake of another. (Let us note, by the way, that the shamanic séance, in which the "descent into Hell" occurs, is equivalent to a mystical experience; the shaman is "outside himself", his soul has left his body.)

Another fundamental shamanic experience is that of the ascent into Heaven: by means of the cosmic Tree planted at the "Centre of the World" the shaman enters into Heaven, where he meets the most high God. All mystics, as we know, make use of the symbolism of ascension to describe the uplifting of the soul and union with God. We should have no right to identify the ascent of the shaman into Heaven with the ascension of the Buddha, of Mohammed or of the Christ: the actual content of these ecstatic experiences is different. This does not prevent the notion of transcendence from expressing itself universally by an Image of elevation: the mystical experience, in whatever religion it may be cradled, always implies a celestial ascension. Furthermore: certain shamanic ecstasies bring about sensations of light which so closely resemble, that they could be mistaken for, similar experiences of the great mystics of history (in India, the Far East, the Mediterranean world, Christianity).

According to the Fathers of the Church, the mystical life consists in a return to Paradise.[10] One of the characteristics of the Paradisiac restoration is to be that dominion over the animals which has hitherto been the privilege of the shamans and of Orpheus. For the re-entry into Paradise reappears among the archaic and primitive mysticisms commonly classed together

[10] See Dom Stoltz, *Théologie de la mystique*; J. Daniélou, *Sacramentum futuri*. It should rather be called an anticipation, for the plenitude of the re-entry into Paradise can be realised only after death.

under the name of shamanism. We have shown elsewhere how
the shaman's trance brings him back into the situation of primordial man. During his trance, the shaman recovers the paradisiac state of the first human beings, who were not separated from
God. Indeed, the traditions tell us of a mythical time when man
was in direct communication with the heavenly gods: by climbing a mountain, a tree, a liana, etc., the First Men could, really
and effortlessly, ascend into Heaven. The gods, for their part,
regularly came down upon earth to mix with men. But after some
mythic event (generally a ritual fault) the communication between
Heaven and Earth was broken (the Tree, the liana, were cut down,
etc.) and the god withdrew into the depths of the sky. (In a
number of traditions the withdrawal of the celestial god is shown
by his ultimate transformation into a *deus otiosus*—an indifferent
god.) But the shaman, by a technique of which he has the secret,
is able—provisionally, and solely for his personal use—to restore
communications with Heaven and resume conversation with
God. In other words, he succeeds in abolishing history (all the
time that has elapsed since the "fall" and the severance of direct
communications between Heaven and Earth); he "returns to the
past", he re-enters the primordial paradisiac condition. This re-
entry into a mythic *illud tempus* happens during the ecstasy; the
shamanic ecstasy may be regarded either as the condition for, or as
the consequence of, a recovery of the paradisiac state. In any case,
it is clear that the mystical experience of the "primitives" also,
is dependent upon the ecstatic re-entry into "Paradise".[11]

This is not to explain Judæo-Christian mysticism by shamanism, nor to identify "shamanic elements" in Christianity. But

[11] One cannot, of course, *reduce* the ecstatic experiences of shamanism to this
"return to Paradise": a number of other elements enter into it. Having devoted
a whole book to this extremely complex problem, I do not think it necessary
here to take up the discussion of it again. Let us note, however, that the shamanic initiation consists of an experience of death and resurrection, a decisive experience that recurs in all the mysticisms in history, including Christian mysticism.

there is one point of an importance that can escape nobody: the mystical experience of the "primitives", like the mystical life of Christians, implies the recovery of the primordial paradisiac condition. *The equivalence of mystical life with the return to Paradise is not, therefore, a unique Judæo-Christian phenomenon created by the intervention of God in history: it is a universal human "datum" of incontestable antiquity.*

Note, here again, that the "intervention of God in history", that is, the divine revelation vouchsafed *in Time*, renews and confirms a "non-temporal situation" The revelation that Judæo-Christianity alone received in a historical time which is never repeated, and which issues in the making of an irreversible history, was already preserved by archaic humanity in mythic form; nevertheless, the mystical experience of the "primitives" as well as the mystical life of Christians expresses itself through this same archetype—the re-entry into the original Paradise. We can clearly see that history—in this case, Sacred History—has brought no innovation. Among the primitives as among Christians, it is always a paradoxical return *in illud tempus*, a "leap backwards" abolishing time and history, that constitutes the mystical re-entry into Paradise. Consequently, although Biblical and Christian symbolism is charged with a historical and—in the last analysis— a "provincial" content (since every local history is provincial in relation to universal history conceived in its totality), it remains nevertheless universal, like every coherent symbolism. We may even wonder whether the accessibility of Christianity may not be attributable in great measure to its symbolism, whether the universal Images that it takes up in its turn have not considerably facilitated the diffusion of its message. For, to the non-Christian, one question occurs first of all: how can a local history—that of the Jewish people and of the first Judæo-Christian communities —how can this claim to have become the pattern for all divine manifestation in concrete, historical Time? I believe we have pointed to the answer: this sacred history, although in the eyes of an alien observer it looks like a local history, is also an exemplary history, because it takes up and perfects these trans-temporal Images.

How, then, are we to account for the irresistible impression, felt by non-Christians especially, that Christianity is an *innovation* in relation to all previous religious life? To a Hindu who is sympathetic to Christianity, the most striking innovation (apart from the message and the divinity of Christ) is its valorisation of Time—in the final reckoning, its *redemption* of Time and of History.[12] Renouncing the reversibility of cyclic Time, it posits a Time that is irreversible, because the hierophanies manifested in it are no longer repeatable: it is once only that the Christ has lived, has been crucified and has been resurrected. Hence a complete fulfilment of the momentary: Time itself is ontologised: Time is made to *be*, which means that it ceases to become, it transforms itself into eternity. But let this be said at once—it is not *any* temporal moment that opens out into eternity, but only the "favourable moment", the instant that is transfigured by a revelation (whether or not we call this "favourable moment" *kāiros*). Time becomes a value, insofar as God manifests himself through it, filling it with a trans-historical meaning and a soteriological intention: for, with each new intervention of God in history, has there not always been a question of the salvation of man—that is, of something which has nothing to do with history? Time turns into pleroma by the very fact of the incarnation of the divine Word: but this fact itself transfigures history. How could it be empty and meaningless—that Time which *saw* Jesus come to birth, suffer, die and rise again? How could it be reversible or repeatable *ad infinitum*?

From the standpoint of the history of religions, Judæo-Christianity presents us with the supreme hierophany: the *transfiguration of the historical event into hierophany*. This means some-

[12] See the lecture by H. C. Puech on "Time, History and Myth in the Christianity of the first centuries" in the *Proceedings of the VIIth Congress on the History of Religions*, Amsterdam, 1951, pp. 33-52; also my *Myth of the Eternal Return*, pp. 102 ff., and Karl Löwith's *Meaning in History*, Chicago, 1949.

thing more than the "hierophanising" of Time, for sacred Time is familiar to all religions. But here it is *the historical event* as such which displays the maximum of trans-historicity: God not only intervenes in history, as in the case of Judaism; he is incarnated in a historic being, in order to undergo a historically conditioned existence. Jesus of Nazareth is, to all appearances, in no way distinguished from his contemporaries in Palestine. Superficially, the Divine is completely concealed in history. Nothing about the physiology, psychology or the "culture" of Jesus gives one any glimpse of God the Father. Jesus eats, digests, suffers from thirst or from the heat, like any other Jew of Palestine. But, in reality, this "historical event" constituted by the existence of Jesus is a total theophany; what it presents is like an audacious effort to *save the historical event* in itself, by endowing it with the maximum of being.

In spite of the value it accords to Time, Judæo-Christianity does not lead to historicism, but to a theology of History. It is not for its own sake that an event is valued, but only for the sake of the revelation it embodies—a revelation that precedes and transcends it. Historicism as such is a product of the decomposition of Christianity: it could only have come about insofar as we had lost faith in the trans-historical reality of the historical event.

One fact, however, remains: Christianity strives to *save* history; first, because it accords a value to historic time; and also because, for the Christian, the historical event, while remaining just what it is, becomes capable of transmitting a trans-historical message. For, since the incarnation of the Christ, the Christian is supposed to look for the interventions of God not only in the Cosmos (with the aid of the cosmic hierophanies, of the Images and symbols), but also in historical events. This is not always an easy undertaking; we may, without too much difficulty, read the "signs" of the divine presence in the Cosmos; but the corresponding "signs" in History are much more disguised.

Indeed, the Christian admits that, after the Incarnation,

miracles are no longer easy to recognise; the greatest of all miracles having been, in fact, the Incarnation itself, all that *which was clearly manifested as miraculous* before Jesus Christ is of no further use or meaning *after* his coming. There is, of course, an uninterrupted series of miracles that the Church accepts, but they have all been validated insofar as they were dependent upon Christ and not for the sake of their intrinsically "miraculous" quality. (We know that the Church carefully distinguishes miracles due to "magic" or to "demons" from those vouchsafed by grace.) The existence and the validity of the miracles accepted by the Church, however, leave open the great problem of the *unrecognisability* of the marvellous in the Christian world; for one may very well find oneself very near to Christ, and *imitate* him, without showing any visible sign of it: one may be *imitating the Christ living his life in history* which, apparently, resembled everybody's existence. Altogether, the Christian is led to approach every historical event with "fear and trembling", since for him even the most commonplace historical event, while continuing to be *real* (that is, historically conditioned) may conceal some new intervention of God in history; in any case it may have a transhistorical meaning, may be charged with a message. Consequently, for the Christian, historical life itself can become glorious—as the life of Christ and the saints bears witness. With the coming of Christianity, it is no longer the Cosmos and the Images only that are able to prefigure and reveal—there is also History, especially that of "everyday life", that which is constituted by events apparently without significance.[13]

[13] The expressions "history" and "historic" can occasion much confusion; they indicate, on the one hand, all that is *concrete* and *authentic* in a given human existence, as opposed to the unauthentic existence constituted by evasions and automatisms of every kind. On the other hand, in the various historicist and existentialist currents of thought, "history" and "historic" seem to imply that human existence is authentic only insofar as it is reduced to the *awakened consciousness of its historic moment*. It is to the latter, the "totalitarian" meaning of history that I am referring when I take issue against "historicisms". It seems to

Undoubtedly. And yet it must not be lost sight of, that Christianity entered into History in order to abolish it: the greatest hope of the Christian is the second coming of Christ, which is to put an end to all History. From a certain point of view, for every Christian individually, this end, and the eternity to follow it—the paradise regained—may be attained *from this moment. The time to come* announced by the Christ is already accessible, and for him who has regained it, history ceases to be. The transformation of Time into Eternity commenced with the first believers. But this paradoxical transformation of Time into Eternity is not the exclusive property of Christianity. We have met with the same conception and the same symbolism in India (see p. 81 above). *Ksana* corresponds to *kāiros*; the one like the other may become the "favourable moment" through which one passes out of time and rejoins eternity . . . The Christian is, in the final reckoning, required to become the contemporary of the Christ: and this implies a concrete existence in history, as well as contemporaneity with the preaching, the agony and the resurrection of the Christ.

SYMBOLS AND CULTURES

The history of a symbolism is a fascinating study, and one that is also fully justified, since it is the best introduction to what is called the philosophy of culture. Images, archetypes and symbols are variously lived and valued; and the product of these multiple realisations of them is largely constitutive of the different "cultural styles" of life. At Ceram, an island in the Molucca Sea, as at

---

me, indeed, that the authenticity of an existence cannot be limited to the consciousness of its own historicity; one cannot regard as "evasive" or "unauthentic", the fundamental experiences of love, anxiety, joy, melancholy, etc. Each of these makes use of a temporal rhythm proper to itself, and all combine to constitute what might be called the *integral man*, who neither denies himself to his historic moment, nor consents to be identified with it.

Eleusis, we again hear of the mythical adventures of a primordial young woman—of Hainuwele, as of Kore Persephone.[14] From the structural point of view, their myths show resemblances— and yet, what a difference between the Greek and the Ceramian cultures! The morphology of culture, the philosophy of styles, will be chiefly concerned with the particular forms taken on by the image of the Young Woman in Greece and in the Moluccan Isles respectively. But although, regarded as historical formations, these cultures are no longer interchangeable, being already fixed in their own styles, they are still comparable upon the plane of imagery and symbolism. It is just this perennial and universal quality of the archetypes which "saves" cultures in the last resort, and renders possible a philosophy of culture that is more than a morphology or history of styles. All culture is a "fall" into history, and is, by the same token, limited. Let no one be misled by the incomparable beauty, nobility and perfection of Greek culture; even this does not make it universally valid *as a historical phenomenon*. Try, for instance, to reveal the Greek culture to an African or to an Indonesian: it is not the admirable Greek "style" that they will understand; it is the Images that the African or Indonesian will rediscover in classical statuary or literature. What is, for an Occidental, *beautiful* and *true* in the *historic manifestation* of antique culture has no value for an Oceanian; for any culture is limited by its manifestation in the structures and styles conditioned by history. But the Images which precede and inform cultures remain eternally alive and universally accessible. A European will find it difficult to admit that the broadly humanist spiritual value and the profound meaning of such a Greek master- piece as the Venus of Milo, for instance, does not reside—for three-quarters of the human race—in the formal perfection of that statue but in the image of Woman which it conveys. Nevertheless, if we do not manage to grasp that simple matter of fact, there is no hope of entering into any useful dialogue with a non-European.

[14] See Ad. E. Jensen, *Hainuwele. Volkserzählungen von der Molukken-Insel Ceram*, Frankfurt-a-Mein, 1939; *id.*, *Die Drei Ströme*, Leipzig, 1948, pp. 277 ff.

After all, it is the presence of the images and symbols that keeps the cultures "open": starting from no matter what culture, the Australian no less than the Athenian, the "limit-situations" of man are fully revealed, owing to the symbols that sustain those cultures. If we neglect this unique spiritual foundation of the various cultural styles, the philosophy of culture will be condemned to remain no more than a morphological and historical study, without any validity for the human condition as such. If the Images were not at the same time an "opening-out" into the transcendent, one would ultimately become suffocated in any culture, however great and admirable one might believe it to be. Starting from any stylistically and historically conditioned creation of the spirit one can regain the vision of the archetype: Kore Persephone, as well as Hainuwele, reveals to us the same pathetic, yet creative destiny of the Young Woman.

The Images provide "openings" into a trans-historical world. That is by no means their least value: thanks to them, the different "histories" can intercommunicate. Much has been said about the unification of Europe by Christianity: and it is never better attested than when we see how Christianity co-ordinated the popular religious traditions. It was by means of Christian hagiography that the local cults—from Thrace to Scandinavia and from the Tagus to the Dnieper—were brought under a "common denominator." By the fact of their Christianisation, the gods and the sacred places of the whole of Europe not only received common names but rediscovered, in a sense, their own archetypes and therefore their universal valencies: a fountain in Gaul, regarded as sacred ever since prehistoric times, but sanctified by the presence of a divine local or regional figure, became sacred *for Christianity as a whole* after its consecration to the Virgin Mary. All the slayers of dragons were assimilated to Saint George or to some other Christian hero; all the Gods of the storm to holy Elijah. From having been regional and provincial, the popular mythology became ecumenical. It is, above all, through the creation of a new mythological language common to all the populations who remained attached to their soil—and therefore in the greater danger of becoming insulated in their own ancestral traditions—that the civilising mission of Christianity has been so remarkable. For, by Christianising the ancient European religious heritage, it not only purified the latter, but took up, into the new spiritual dispensation of mankind, all that deserved to be "saved" of the old practices, beliefs and hopes of pre-Christian man. Even today, in popular Christianity, there are rites and beliefs surviving from the neolithic: the boiled grain in honour of the dead, for instance (the *coliva* of Eastern and Ægean Europe). The Christianisation of the peasant levels of Europe was effected thanks above all to the Images: everywhere they were rediscovered, and had only to be revalorised, reintegrated and given new names.

Let us not hope, however, for an analogous phenomenon tomorrow, repeated upon the planetary scale. On the contrary, the reaction that will be provoked everywhere by the entry of the exotic peoples into history will be a heightening of the prestige of the autochthonous religions. As we have said, the West is now compelled to accept a dialogue with the other, the "exotic" or "primitive" cultures. It would be regrettable indeed if we entered upon this without having learnt anything from all the revelations vouchsafed to us by the study of symbolisms.

REMARKS UPON METHOD

One can see, after what has just been said, the sense in which we have now gone beyond the "confusionist" position of a Tylor or a Frazer, who, in their anthropological and ethnographical researches, accumulated examples which had no geographical or historical contiguity, and would cite an Australian myth together with one from Siberia, Africa or North America, persuaded as they were that always and everywhere they were dealing with the same "uniform reaction of the human mind before the phenomena of Nature". Compared with this position, so similar to that of a naturalist of the Darwinian epoch, the historico-cultural school of Graebner-Schmidt and the other historicist schools represent an undeniable progress. It was important, however, not to let ourselves become fixed in the historico-cultural point of view, and to inquire whether, in addition to its own history, a symbol, a myth or a ritual, might not reveal something of the human condition regarded in its own right as a mode of existence in the universe. That is what I have tried to do here, and in several other recent publications.[15]

Tylor and Frazer, like good positivists, regarded the magico-religious life of archaic humanity as a mass of childish "superstitions", the product of ancestral fears or of "primitive" stupidity. But that value-judgment is in contradiction to the facts. The magico-religious behaviour of archaic humanity reveals an existential awakening of man's consciousness of the Cosmos and of himself. Here, where a Frazer could see nothing but "superstition", a metaphysic was already implicit, even though it was expressed by a pattern of symbols rather than by the interplay of concepts: a metaphysic—that is, a whole and coherent conception of Reality, not a series of instinctive gestures ruled by the same fundamental "reaction of the human animal in confrontation with Nature". Thus when, leaving on one side the "history" that divides them, we compare an Oceanian symbol with a symbol from Northern Asia, we think we are entitled to do so, not because both the one and the other are products of the same "infantile mentality", but because the symbol in itself expresses an awakening to the knowledge of a "limit-situation".

Attempts have been made to explain the "origin" of symbols by sensory impressions, made directly upon the cerebral cortex, by the great cosmic rhythms (the path of the Sun, for instance). It is not our business to discuss that hypothesis. But the problem of "the origin" seems to us to be, in itself, a problem badly stated (see above, p. 119). Symbols cannot be reflections of cosmic rhythms *as natural phenomena*, for a symbol always reveals some-

[15] This problem will be fully discussed in the second volume of my *Patterns in Comparative Religion*.

thing *more* than the aspect of cosmic life it is thought to represent. The solar symbolisms and myths, for example, reveal to one also a "nocturnal", "evil" and "funerary" aspect of the Sun, something that is not at first *evident* in the solar phenomenon as such. This—in a sense negative—side, which is not perceived in the Sun *as a cosmic phenomenon*, is constitutive in the solar *symbolism*, which proves that the symbol arises, from the beginning, as a creation of the psyche. This becomes still more evident when we remember that the function of a symbol is precisely that of revealing a whole reality, inaccessible to other means of knowledge: the coincidence of opposites, for instance, which is so abundantly and *simply* expressed by symbols, is not *given* anywhere in the *Cosmos*, nor is it accessible to man's immediate experience, nor to discursive thinking.

Let us beware, however, of supposing that symbolism refers only to "spiritual" realities. For to archaic thinking, such a separation between the "spiritual" and the "material" is without meaning: the two planes are complementary. The fact that a dwelling house is supposed to be at "the Centre of the World" does not make it any the less a convenience which answers to specific needs and is conditioned by the climate, the economic structure of society and the architectural tradition. Recently, the old quarrel has broken out again between the "symbolists" and the "realists" in reference to the religious architecture of ancient Egypt. But the two positions are only apparently irreconcilable: within the horizons of archaic mentality, taking account of "immediate realities" does not in the least mean that one is ignorant or contemptuous of their symbolic implications, or *vice versa*. It must not be thought that the symbolical application annuls the concrete and specific value of an object or an operation. When the spade is called a phallus (as it happens to be in certain Australasian languages) and when the sowing is likened to the sexual act (as it has been almost all over the world), it does not follow that the "primitive" agriculturist is ignorant of the specific purpose of his labour or of the concrete, practical value of that

tool. The symbolism *adds* a new value to an object or an activity
without any prejudice whatever to its own immediate value. In
application to objects or actions, symbolism renders them
"open"; symbolic thinking "breaks open" the immediate reality
without any minimising or undervaluing of it: in such a perspective this is not a closed Universe, no object exists for itself in
isolation; everything is held together by a compact system of
correspondences and likenesses.[16] The man of the archaic societies
becomes conscious of himself in an "open world" that is rich in
meaning. It remains to be seen whether these "openings" are but
so many means of evasion, or whether, on the contrary, they
constitute the only possibility of attaining to the true reality of
the world.

[16] Rightly to understand the transformation of the world by the symbol, one
need only recall the dialectic of hierophany: an object becomes *sacred* while remaining just the same as it is. (See above, p. 84.)

INDEX

For method paper: p.27,
p. 33